BITE BUSTERS

BITE BUSTERS

How to deal with dog attacks

Sylvia Wilson

SIMON & SCHUSTER
AUSTRALIA

Important note: The techniques used in this book should be practised with your own, other people's and the dog's safety uppermost
in your mind. The author and publisher accept no responsibility
for any loss, damage, injury or inconvenience sustained by any
person or pet as a result of using the methods outlined herein.

BITE BUSTERS

First published in Australasia in 1997 by
Simon & Schuster Australia
20 Barcoo Street, East Roseville NSW 2069

Viacom International
Sydney New York London Toronto Tokyo Singapore

National Library of Australia
Cataloguing-in-Publication data

Wilson, Sylvia
    Bite busters : how to deal with dog attacks.

    ISBN 0 7318 0619 0.

    1. Dogs – Behaviour. 2. Dogs – Training. 3. Aggressive
    behaviour in animals. I. Title.

636.70887

Designed by Aartworks
Illustrations by Robyn Cunningham
Printed in Australia by McPherson's Print Group

This book is dedicated to my husband, Danny, who has believed in me from the start. His undying enthusiasm and love of dogs has been instrumental in the success of our company, Bark Busters, and the dog safety program Stand Right No Bite.

I am a technician for an electricity company. One day without warning, I was attacked. The following months were mentally agonising for me. I couldn't do my work if there was a dog on the premises. Thanks to the Stand Right No Bite program, I respect the danger in an attack situation, but can now control it, as I have done in two attacks since my training.

Todd Barclay

Foreword

As a veterinary surgeon, I am often approached to give my approval of some new product or technique. More often than not I politely decline, aghast at the principle or theory behind the idea. It was therefore with a sense of trepidation that I agreed to read and then comment on Sylvia's book on how to deal with dog attacks. Happily, it is a book where commonsense prevails. It debunks the myths and exposes the old wives' tales that cause me so much hassle and grief in my daily duties at work. I have long realised, as a woman vet, that brute force and confrontation are rarely, if ever, the correct way to interact with any animal — large or small. Greater success is usually achieved by understanding how my patient is interpreting the situation and playing by pack rules, along with a liberal dose of blarney and bribery by way of treats.

Many euthanasias on dogs are due in no small part to the human at the other end of the lead completely misreading the situation and expecting their beloved pet to be beyond reproach. I often hear owners who say their dog is wonderful with kids and would never bite. But *all* dogs, given the right set of circumstances, will bite and we have a duty to be aware of those situations and avoid the unnecessary stress to the pet and grief to ourselves. Sylvia's book goes a long way to informing us of those situations, how to avoid them where possible and what to do should we find ourselves in an attack situation.

Bite Busters makes excellent and easy reading and is a must for vet students and nurses, meter readers, dog owners and anyone who comes into regular contact with dogs. Empowered with an alternative view to some of the current theories on dog control, readers will enjoy a safer and more rewarding daily interaction with their four-legged friend.

Just remember, as Sylvia says, humans smack with their hands, dogs smack with their mouths, and while we may fail to be consistent in our application of the laws of the pack, our beloved pet will not.

Aine Seavers MRCVS, MVB

Contents

Part 3: Handling dogs safely: a guide for professionals

Acknowledgments

With special thanks to:

All those who believed in and encouraged the development of this book, particularly the Bark Busters licensees throughout Australia who shared many wonderful stories with me.

Integral Energy and Energy Australia for their faith and support, and for helping launch the Stand Right No Bite dog safety program.

Healthy Cities Wollongong, who invited us to participate in their Stop-A-Bite program.

Todd Barclay and the Total Quality Team at Energy Australia.

Aine Seavers MRCVS, MVB, one of Australia's most competent and caring vets, for the wonderful Foreword and for sharing my long-held beliefs.

Introduction

Every day I come across alarming reports in the media of someone who has been attacked by a dog. Horrific stories of people who are permanently disfigured or children who are maimed for life, simply because they were trying to pat a dog and make friends. Stories about the trauma suffered by the victims of attacks; once normal, happy individuals who now break out in a cold sweat and start shaking at the sound of a dog's bark.

As one of the founders and directors of Bark Busters home dog training, I have now been investigating the dog attack problem for eight years. By speaking to numerous people who have been attacked and to owners whose dogs have attacked others, I have been able to put together many of their stories and have attempted to understand why they were attacked and how the attack could have been avoided.

To avoid being attacked or bitten by dogs we first need to understand *why* they attack. In my experience as a dog therapist and trainer, and as the former manager of a busy RSPCA shelter for ten years, I've learnt one thing — a dog won't bite you if you do the right thing. Don't act like you are afraid. Running away, moving about, behaving aggressively and even normal reflex actions, will encourage an aggressive dog to attack. I've discovered, through my Bark Busters dog safety program — Stand Right No Bite — that people can be trained to understand how dogs think and relate to certain human body language and the reason why dogs bite. Knowing this, they are able to reduce the risk of being attacked.

I speak to numerous people in the course of my work, many of whom have to enter homes and properties on a regular basis as part of their job. Some have a genuine fear of dogs, and their actions increase the likelihood of being bitten; others come into contact with guard dogs and vicious dogs regularly and, like myself, never get bitten. I believe this is because they have a healthy respect for the dogs they meet and are aware of the 'rules'. They always behave in a proper manner around dogs and do only those things that dogs feel comfortable with.

As I write this, I am looking at a picture in the *Australian Women's Weekly* of a woman whose lip was bitten off by a dog while she was trying to perform her normal everyday duties, which involved visiting people's homes. A court finally awarded her $55,000 compensation for her ordeal. That might sound like a lot of money, but the woman in question had to resign from her job because she could no longer visit homes for fear of being attacked. Apart from being disfigured for life, she was now unemployed as well.

Part of the reason we are hearing more and more stories of seemingly unpredictable and unjustified attacks is largely to do with the way society is forced to keep its dogs. Local councils are constantly introducing tough new laws aimed at totally isolating the domestic dog. In addition, many people want their family pet to function as a watchdog, that protects their property while they are out at work, which means the dog is left alone for hours on end.

Although I don't think that dogs should be allowed to run wild in the streets, and understand that councils need to take a tough stand on the dog problem, it's this isolation that is partly to blame for the increase in dog attacks.

What is the answer? How do we protect ourselves and our families from a dog attack? The answer is simple. Understand the reasons why people get bitten and how it could have been avoided. Learn the right way to react in a potentially dangerous situation with a dog.

With education and a clear understanding of what makes a dog attack, I feel it's possible for each and every one of us to avoid being attacked or bitten by a dog.

Part 1

Why dogs bite

THE MODERN-DAY DOG

The dog has been domesticated for at least 10,000 years, and over that time it has changed quite dramatically. Today there are over one hundred breeds, all of which are the result of selective breeding to make them suitable for various tasks (for example, hunting, herding, guarding). However, despite their different appearances, all dogs belong to the same species — *Canis familiaris*. The dog's most recent ancestor is thought to be the grey wolf; indeed, the German shepherd, the malamute and the Siberian husky still resemble the wolf.

In the wild, dogs live in packs. They are social creatures and do not adapt well to an independent life. This is one of the reasons they make such wonderful family pets — the family serves as the pack. However, regardless of selective breeding and domestication, we cannot erase those wild instincts that pulse through their veins.

A friend of mine lives on a large property in the Hills District of Sydney, and although her many dogs are well fed, they still go off rabbiting when the urge takes them. I guess if fate dealt them a cruel blow and they became lost, they would be able to survive quite well without human assistance because nature has provided them with the instinct to hunt for their food.

Another woman I know had a dog that joined a wild pack of dogs which was marauding at the top corner of her huge property. It appears that her dog lacked leadership — which all dogs need — so went in search of a leader.

In my experience, domestic dogs have the ability to revert to the wild if the need arises. Very young puppies still protect their food in the same way their ancestors did thousands of years ago. Female dogs giving birth still growl and snarl at their mate if he enters the whelping area. Dogs still bark to summon the pack and ward off strangers, and will attack if necessary. Dogs that are free to roam still chase and kill and form packs.

The dog's instinct to form packs and to protect its den or territory from other marauding packs or predators is vital to its survival in the wild. The modern domesticated dog is also governed by pack instinct. There is one leader and other members of the pack fall into place in order of dominance.

There are times when a dominant dog will attack a subordinate dog. This usually happens because the inferior dog has overstepped the line and has done something that the dominant dog considered a threat to its superior position. In most cases the subordinate dog will submit immediately, leaving nothing more to fight about. However, if the dog that is under attack panics and keeps fighting, the fight will continue until one of the dogs is either severely injured or dead.

A subordinate dog will usually never attack a dog that is higher up the pecking order. When this does occur, although somewhat rare, the fight is of a very serious nature.

A dog's body language is important in staving off attack from other dogs. Some dogs will adopt a submissive pose and roll over on to their back, exposing their throat and lying still. Other, more confidant dogs will stiffen up completely, freezing their movements. All of these signals are taken by the aggressor to mean that the other dog is no threat.

INSTINCT AND AGGRESSION

Contrary to popular belief, most dogs would prefer *not* to bite humans. The Australian Police Dog Squad rejects a large percentage of the potential police dogs they test. The dogs are not suitable for many reasons, ranging from medical soundness and fitness to timidity, but one of the main reasons is that the majority of dogs they test are *reluctant to bite*. This ability to bite is extremely important in a police dog which needs to use its mouth to effect an arrest for its handler.

Given this natural reluctance to bite, why are more and more people getting bitten? The reasons are numerous. First, there are more dogs in our society than ever before and, for the most part, we are made to keep them isolated. Local councils are constantly introducing tougher legislation which insists that owners confine their dogs. Even though I agree that this is necessary, I feel it partly explains the increase in dog attacks, primarily because years ago, dogs were free to roam the streets and were able to socialise with other dogs as a result. A socialised dog is normally a friendly dog, whereas an isolated dog can become fearful, which can lead to aggressive behaviour.

Another reason for dog attacks is that most people don't understand what motivates a dog to attack and how their body language can incite a dog to attack. They are unaware that their actions may indicate aggressive tendencies or that the way they behave when a dog looks like it's going to bite them can lead the dog to believe it is under attack or that its quarry is scared and therefore easy prey.

Dogs are not able to think and reason in the same way we can; they do not have human logic. Instead, their behaviour is mostly guided by *memory* and *instinct*. Often when a dog bites, it is doing so out of instinct. There are numerous reasons for this, which are discussed below. I have drawn parallels between human and canine behaviour so that you can better understand a dog's motivations.

Fear

Fear is a powerful survival instinct. If something scares a dog, it will do one of two things: run away or stay and fight. This is known as the *fight or flight response,* and it is common to all animals.

Fear is a powerful survival instinct, and a dog that has had no contact with strangers or has suffered at the hands of a human is more likely to become aggressive out of fear.

A dog that has had no contact with strangers or has had a bad experience at the hands of a human is much more likely to attack than a dog that loves people and has had only good experiences with them.

I mentioned in the introduction a woman who had been severely traumatised by a dog attack and how some people who've been attacked break out in a cold sweat and shake at the sound of a dog's bark. These are logical, thinking people who prior to the attack possibly had many good experiences with dogs, yet one bad experience has scarred them for life. They are now afraid of all dogs. A dog can react to a bad experience in a similar way, but the difference is it may become aggressive out of fear.

The following case history shows how one bad experience can turn an angel into a monster.

Case history: When I first met Brutus, a Belgian shepherd, he was a terrifying sight. I first glimpsed his staring, mad eyes through a crack in a wooden gate, which was threatening to burst because he would launch himself at it in an effort to get at whoever was on the other side. His frightening appearance was surpassed only by his bloodcurdling bark, which would have scared even the bravest of people.

I had been called in by Jenny, his owner, to cure her dog's aggression. When I entered the house, I was able to watch Brutus from the safety of the kitchen window, which gave me a good view of his domain – the backyard.

Jenny told me his story. Brutus was only an eight-week-old puppy when Jenny's next-door neighbour – whom Brutus had never met – entered the yard to retrieve a ball that he'd accidentally hit over the fence. Another dog was in the yard at the time and was raiding the garbage bin. When the neighbour spotted the strange dog, he raised his cricket bat above his head and ran at it screaming, sending the dog and garbage bin flying. The dog bolted over the fence leaving a terrified Brutus trapped in his yard, petrified by what he had just witnessed.

As Jenny related this story, I visualised a frightened pup, a novice, unsure of the ways of the human world he had just entered. All he knew of humans other than his owner was that they were to be feared and not under any circumstances to be let into the yard. Any previous good experiences Brutus had had with humans were totally annihilated that day, in much the same way some people react once attacked by a dog.

Brutus had grown to hate all people other than Jenny from that day on. His main purpose in life was to get humans before they got him. As I stood in the kitchen that day, watching Brutus jumping and leaping at the window trying to get at me, I couldn't help but feel sorry for him. His actions were based on fear – the flight or fight response. And Brutus had decided to fight.

Territoriality

Territoriality is defined in the *Macquarie Dictionary* as 'the behaviour of an animal in claiming and defending its territory'. In the definition of territory it says, 'the area which an animal or pair of animals claim as their own and defend against intruders'.

The ancestors of the modern-day dog had to defend the areas in which they lived and hunted. The area they chose would have largely depended on its resources. They would

Dogs are territorial animals and will defend an area they consider to be their own. This means that if you enter a dog's backyard without due caution, you could be bitten.

have needed shelter from the sun and rain, and easy access to a watering hole or spring. Caves, or rocks under which they could dig dens, would possibly have been an important factor, providing the female of the species with a suitable place for whelping. The instinct to protect their territory was essential to their survival.

This same instinct is still very strong in some domestic dogs, even though we provide for most of their needs. If a dog considers an area to be its territory and you step into that area, then you could be in trouble if you don't know the rules.

The size of the area a dog will defend largely depends on the dog and whether it is allowed to roam the streets or is confined to a backyard. The following case history highlights why you may be attacked if you act the wrong way around a territorial dog.

Case history: As part of his job, David visited other people's homes on a regular basis. The one thing he disliked intensely about his work was dogs. Even though he had two of his own, David was afraid of dogs. He'd had more than one close shave when confronted by them.

David had recently had an operation on his knee and was walking with the aid of a walking stick – on this particular day he was also carrying a large bag. He came to a house that was fully enclosed by a fence, with a large double gate at the entrance. He went through the gate, closing it behind him. He froze momentarily when he heard a dog bark, but continued down the path, thinking the dog was locked inside. At that moment, a bull terrier popped out from under the house. David stopped in his tracks; the hairs stood up on the back of his neck and he broke into a cold sweat.

He wanted to run, but the gate was closed and too far away. He knew he would never make it. The dog trotted up to him, barking. Fearing an attack, David thrust his bag straight into the unsuspecting dog's face. The dog grabbed the bag in its jaws and they were locked in a tussle.

David tried unsuccessfully to get his bag back. Although he wanted to get out of there, he was not going to leave without his bag. But no matter how hard he pulled, the dog would not let go. Up until this point David had not received any injuries, other than to his pride.

He looked around but there was no one in sight. No one to help him out of this predicament. Mustering his courage, David decided to take action.

Lifting his walking stick above his head, he brought it down forcefully on the bull terrier's head. The dog let go of the bag and attacked David with all the force and frenzy it could muster. His worst nightmares had come true: he was under attack. The dog was going berserk, attacking David with such force that he was knocked to the ground. The dog was now on top of him. He attempted to cover his face with his hands but the dog was biting every limb that moved. David was fighting for his life.

Suddenly, the dog's owner appeared from inside the house and, grabbing its collar, pulled the dog off him. The owner locked the dog away and rang for an ambulance.

David was taken to hospital suffering from shock and with 47 puncture wounds to his legs, arms and upper torso. The dog's owner was at a loss to understand what had happened as his dog had never bitten anyone before.

Some of you might think that this was a particularly aggressive and unprovoked attack, and that the dog should have been declared dangerous. I admit that the attack was vicious, but let's look at it more closely.

Here was a normally friendly dog that barked as a stranger entered its yard. (In the wild dogs bark to summon the pack, not as a prelude to an attack.) It trotted up to David, barking as it went, then suddenly a bag was thrust in its face. It grabbed the bag, no doubt to stop it from being thrust in its face again. The dog was then attacked with a walking stick, again in its own yard. The rest is known.

Now let's look at the same scenario, but with people rather than dogs. Just imagine you are at home when you hear a noise and notice a stranger entering your property. You run towards him saying, 'Hey! What do you want?' Suddenly a bag is thrust in your face. You grab it, to ensure it doesn't happen again. Then you are hit over the head with a walking stick. How would you react?

When lecturing on dog safety, I often ask the class to imagine for a moment that they are in a locked cell with only one way out. A mad axeman is coming towards them, blocking the exit. I then ask them what would they do. The answer is usually unanimous. They say they will fight.

Unfortunately, a dog cannot stop and ask questions, it can only draw on its instincts. Instinct tells it that, if in danger, it has two options: fight for its life or run like mad. A dog that has spent its life in a fenced yard that it has never been able to escape from, except perhaps when its owner has taken it out, does not go for the 'run like mad' option.

Food protection

In the wild, a dog's survival largely depended on the food supply. The instinct to protect this supply often meant the difference between life and death. Puppies that did not push

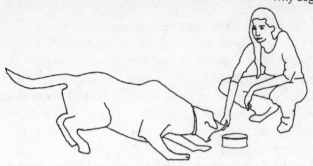

Food aggression is the cause of many attacks on dog owners. The dog should be trained not to behave this way from the time it is a puppy.

and shove to defend their meal usually perished. Domestic dogs learn very early on that they need to push and fight to get the lion's share of the food, especially in large litters of puppies. When a breeder places either one large or two smaller bowls of food on the ground and encourages a 'free for all' amongst a large litter of puppies, they run the risk of creating food-aggressive dogs. This is because it creates panic and stress in the pups. They feel they might miss out, so they push and growl at each other. Because dogs are creatures of habit, this behaviour is then carried on when a pup is relocated in a new home and into its adult life. It feels it needs to fight for its food and its owner could be bitten if they get in the way.

The ideal way to feed pups is separately or in twos, and to separate the pups from the other litter mates during feeding. This creates a much calmer atmosphere and the pups do not feel pressured to eat.

Case history: Years ago when I was managing an RSPCA shelter, a woman brought in an aged German shepherd named Sasha. She was distraught and asked me if I would euthanise her pet immediately. Because the dog appeared to be very healthy and happy, I asked her why she felt it necessary to have her pet put to sleep. She explained that she loved Sasha very much and that the dog had once saved her life when she almost drowned in the surf. So what had led her to arrive at this horrendous decision?

She went on to tell me that the day before, her fourteen-year-old son had entered their backyard and attempted to lean his bike up against a tree when Sasha viciously attacked him, inflicting some severe wounds on his face. The whole family was in shock. None of them felt they could trust a dog that had suddenly turned on one of the family.

My inquiring, investigative mind would not let me leave it at that, so I prodded the woman for more information.

Had Sasha ever bitten a member of the family before? No.

Could she think of any reason for the attack? No.

Had Sasha known it was her son entering the yard?

This time the answer was 'yes'. The woman's son had said Sasha greeted him in her usual way, happy and with tail wagging. She only became aggressive when he attempted to lean his bike against the tree.

I had now heard something that prompted my next question: Was Sasha food aggressive? The woman looked puzzled. I elaborated: Was Sasha aggressive if anyone went near her food or when she was eating?

The woman appeared not to understand what I was getting at, though she nodded. 'Yes, she is food aggressive. She snarls if she has food or a bone, but we all know that and stay away from her when she is eating. But this had nothing to do with food. She wasn't eating at the time.'

At this point, I took hold of Sasha's lead and said to the woman, 'I want you to go home and dig around that tree and let me know what you find. I won't do anything with Sasha until I hear back from you.'

The woman returned an hour later and as she started to speak, tears filled her eyes. 'You were right,' she said. 'I found a bone I had given her the other day, which I thought she had finished, buried right near where my son was going to lean his bike. What will I do? My husband and family are adamant they don't want to take any more chances with Sasha. My son has fifteen stitches in his face and will be scarred for life.'

'The choice has to be yours,' I said. 'I cannot tell you what to do with your dog, I can only explain why it happened and give you some advice on how best to prevent the situation from happening again.'

The woman left Sasha with me, desperately torn between her family and the dog she loved so much.

Sasha was eventually put to sleep: her owner phoned and said she could not trust Sasha enough to take her home again. The RSPCA could not pass on a dog of Sasha's age or reputation as other people would have been at risk without training, and Sasha's training would have been better carried out by those she had loved and trusted for so long.

Sasha's attack could have been prevented if her owners had sought professional advice and training to cure her food aggression. The attack upon the fourteen-year-old boy might not have happened if Sasha's owners had been less tolerant of their dog's bad behaviour.

Self-preservation

Self-preservation simply means looking after yourself, protecting yourself from harm. When it comes to the animal kingdom, the instinct for self-preservation is very powerful. An animal will protect itself tenaciously when it feels threatened. The only time it will ignore its own wellbeing is when protecting its offspring. In this case, certain animals will try to draw predators away from their offspring or attack viciously in an effort to protect them.

When citing self-preservation as a reason for domestic dog attacks, we have to keep in mind that we are dealing with a simple creature which has no understanding of the ways of the human world and yet lives closely with humans.

I am sure if Sasha had known that by attacking her mistress's son she had signed her own death warrant, she would not have done it. She was doing something instinctive to preserve her life, not destroy it. Obviously, she had no idea what her actions on that day would lead to.

With that in mind, the following case history tells the story of a dog that attacked because it felt its life was in danger.

Case history: A labrador named Chester, who spent a great deal of his life tied to a kennel, was the perpetrator of an horrendous attack upon his owner's next-door neighbour. The neighbour had hit Chester with a stick on many occasions, thrown rocks at him and hosed him over the fence when Chester's owners were out, all in an attempt to quell Chester's frantic barking. Chester had come to fear this man, but had no way of avoiding the onslaught. All the efforts the neighbour made to stop his barking only resulted in making Chester bark more out of fear for his life.

The tables turned dramatically one Christmas Eve when the neighbour was a guest at Chester's owner's house. Having had one too many, he staggered into the yard to relieve himself, totally forgetting about Chester. Lying inside his kennel and hidden by the darkness, Chester must have recognised the man's footsteps and voice as he mumbled something to himself and fumbled with his clothing. Chester tensed himself, fearing another beating.

Waiting until the man was within reach of his chain, Chester pounced, grabbing the man on the buttocks. The man leapt forward, pulling himself free from Chester's jaws, but Chester then sunk his teeth into the man's calf and this time he was not letting go. The man fell to the ground screaming. Suddenly, the lights went on in the garden and Chester's owner appeared on the scene. It took the owner and two other guests at the party to prise the man's leg from Chester's jaws.

The man refused all efforts by the owner to take him to hospital and would not hear of Chester being punished for the attack. He said it was his fault and a few days later even confessed to Chester's owner what he had been doing to the dog.

A week later, Chester was destroyed. His owner felt he was too dangerous and unpredictable. Even in light of what the owner had been told by his neighbour, what he'd witnessed had really scared him, and no amount of pleading by his neighbour could convince Chester's owner to give him a stay of execution.

Protection of mate/offspring/owner

Many dog attacks occur because people either come too close to whatever the dog is protecting or inadvertently threaten one of the things the dog holds dear. In the wild, a dog relies heavily on the pack for its survival. The pack provides food, companionship, social structure and security. It is therefore in the dog's own interest to protect pack members. Because a dog looks upon its owner as part of its pack, it can become protective of them and other members of the family if it believes they are being threatened.

Our family dog, Bullseye, who by nature loves and befriends everyone and appears to have no aggressive tendencies, surprised me one day when he tried to come to the aid of my husband, Danny, who was engaged in some amicable sparring with a friend.

Female dogs instinctively protect their puppies and will defend them against anything they consider to be a threat — including you!

15

Bullseye obviously believed Danny was in danger. If Danny had not acted quickly by grabbing the dog's collar and vocally reprimanding him, I feel sure Bullseye would have bitten our friend. Given the right circumstances, any dog can bite.

Most mothers, whether human or animal, have a natural inclination to protect their offspring. This instinct is nature's way of protecting that particular species. I remember trying to lead my German shepherd Monty into the garden to see his puppies and the reluctance he displayed as we approached the kennel where my female dog Sheba was nursing his offspring. No one was more surprised than me when she flew out of the kennel and attacked him. He knew the rules and from that day on so did I. Sheba was quite happy for me to visit the pups, but for Monty it was out of bounds.

Medical problems

In much the same way that someone's personality can change because of certain medical problems or complications, so too can a dog's. Distemper can lead to dramatic personality changes because the disease attacks the brain and can cause the afflicted dog to hallucinate. Brain tumours and rabies (though rabies is not a problem in Australia) can affect a dog's disposition. A dog's temperament can also change for hormonal reasons, such as when a bitch is in season.

> **Case history:** I was asked to assess the behaviour of a springer spaniel named Bouncer, because his owner, Teresa, was becoming very concerned about his unpredictable temperament. He would be sleeping one minute, and the next he would jump up and bite someone if they walked past, then just as quickly go back to sleep.

Teresa could not think of anything that might have caused Bouncer's strange behaviour. It's as if he were a completely different dog. There were times when he was definitely his normal, lovable self, but then, for no apparent reason, something in his mind would snap and he wouldn't respond to any of her commands.

I listened carefully to Teresa's description of the things Bouncer had been doing and then asked her to take me into the yard to see him. He came up to us wagging his tail, his tongue lolling in his mouth. He appeared to be a very friendly, pleasant and accepting dog.

I decided to put him through some simple exercises to see if he had normal reactions to everything I asked him to do. He became excited when I took my lead out of my bag. I had planned to walk him around the yard first and see just how he would respond to me. He was very affectionate and I began to understand what Teresa was talking about. Here was a loving dog that would not normally be aggressive. There had to be something beyond his control that was making him behave unpredictably.

Suddenly, Bouncer did something very unusual – he hooked both of his front legs around my legs as if to stop me moving forward. Other dogs had done that to me before, but usually they were not lead-trained or were unsure of what I was doing. Bouncer did not fall into either category. He seemed to be trying to tell me something. I crouched down and patted his head, fondling his soft ears. He snuggled into me and I looked into his eyes. What I saw there told me that this dog had something seriously wrong with him.

I turned to Teresa and told her she should get Bouncer to a vet as soon as possible. I thought perhaps he had a mild dose of distemper or a brain tumour. I am not a vet, and my opinion was based on intuition more than anything else. Bouncer never displayed any aggression while I was around, but there definitely appeared to be something wrong with him that you could not quite put your finger on.

Teresa rang me two weeks later to tell me that Bouncer had been diagnosed with a brain tumour. His condition had worsened and he had become very aggressive towards all members of Teresa's family. His attacks became more ferocious and more regular, so Teresa had him put to sleep.

I shed a silent tear when I remembered the way Bouncer seemed to be trying to tell me that he was suffering. I will never forget the look in that dog's eyes.

Although these type of medical conditions are quite rare, they do occur. I have heard of at least half a dozen cases in the past five years, all of which resulted in the dogs being destroyed.

ARE CERTAIN BREEDS MORE AGGRESSIVE?

I am often asked why some dogs are more aggressive than others, and why certain breeds are considered more likely to attack. A survey conducted in South Australia listed the following breeds as those most responsible for attacks on children:

- Bull terrier
- Cattle dog
- Collie
- Doberman
- German shepherd
- Rottweiler

As you read this book, you will notice that several of these dogs feature in the case histories. However, I am not convinced that this means they are more dangerous than other breeds. Indeed, the figures could just be reflecting the fact that they are among the most *popular* breeds, therefore statistically responsible for a greater proportion of attacks.

It is my belief that aggression in a dog has less to do with its breed than its upbringing, initial training, individual temperament, how responsible its owner is and how much training the dog is given. All dogs can be trained. Greyhounds can be trained not to chase, cattle dogs not to herd, hunting dogs not to hunt and fighting dogs not to fight.

Of course, the breed of dog does have a bearing on how serious an attack would be. *The more formidable the breed, the more serious the attack.* Below I discuss those breeds which are often perceived to be aggressive and menacing.

American pit bull terriers

American pit bull terriers are often accused of serious attacks on people. Once they have the victim in their jaws, they shake them from side to side, and do not let go. There are comparatively few pit bulls in Australia, yet they have been responsible for several fatal attacks. However, because they are perceived to be aggressive, vicious dogs, partly due to media hype, there are occasions when they are wrongly blamed for these attacks. At present, there is pressure from various groups calling for the government to enforce a total ban on pit bulls.

I cannot totally condemn this type of thinking, as I can see the reasons for banning particular breeds. On the other hand, I have met and trained some very sensitive and sweet-natured pit bulls — they are not all depraved killers.

The ancestry of the pit bull includes many formidable breeds: the English bull terrier, the Rhodesian ridgeback, the bull mastiff and the Staffordshire bull terrier, amongst others. Originally they were bred to fight other dogs, never people. In fact, all fighting dogs were bred to be loyal and friendly towards humans, otherwise they would have been impossible to handle.

Like any breed, some pit bulls can be aggressive, and if so they are extremely dangerous because of their size, strength and fighting capability. Others are friendly by nature, but have been encouraged by an irresponsible owner to become aggressive.

English bull terriers

The English bull terrier was originally bred to herd bulls, in an effort to find a dog that was faster and more agile than the bulldog. Its ancestry includes the British bulldog, the fox terrier and the Dalmatian.

English bull terrier

Because of its tenacity, fearlessness and powerful jaws, the bull terrier was later used as a fighting dog. Like any dog that was bred to fight other dogs, the bull terrier is very determined and tenacious. It had to be strong and able to grab the other dog and hang on with its powerful jaws, regardless of any injury to itself or the size and strength of its opponent. This tenacity was also one of the reasons it was so successful at herding bulls. Bulls are extremely stubborn creatures, unpredictable and easy to anger. They would have had no hesitation retaliating and attacking with their horns, goring the dog or sending it flying through the air.

Bull terriers were not bred to attack people, and in fact they make loyal and lovable family pets. They are trusted and cherished by many dog owners, including myself. They do have a tendency to be aggressive towards other dogs, however, but if they are well trained and closely controlled, this does not usually present a problem.

German shepherds

The German shepherd is, essentially, a sheepdog, though it was bred to guard sheep and prevent them straying from a particular area rather than to herd them. Unlike dogs that were specifically bred to herd cattle, sheepdogs have no need to be

German shepherd

forceful or overly aggressive. They mostly bark and snap to get the sheep to do what they want them to.

If a German shepherd attacks a person, it will usually bite quickly and then let go. This method of attack is unlike that of the 'bull' breeds, which do not let go of their quarry once they have it in their jaws.

Although shepherds can be somewhat aloof and suspicious of strangers, they are very friendly to those they trust and make wonderful family pets, providing they are trained from an early age. A loyal and loving companion, the German shepherd is by far one of the most popular breeds — not only as family pets but as police dogs and guides for the blind as well.

Note: Like German shepherds, collies are sheepdogs, and in attack situations their approach is similar.

Staffordshire bull terriers

The Staffordshire bull terrier — affectionately known as a staffy — is becoming increasingly popular as a family pet, and has a reputation for being particularly good with children. Descended from the bulldog and various breeds of terrier, it was originally bred to fight other dogs — a task the

21

staffy excelled at because, like the pit bull, once it attacks it does not let go.

Staffordshire bull terriers are strong, muscular and agile, but they possess an amiable nature and are rarely aggressive towards humans. In fact, they are renowned for their loyalty and devotion to their owners.

Rhodesian ridgebacks

The Rhodesian ridgeback hails from Africa, where it was bred to fight and hunt lions. A dog of immense strength, it has very powerful jaws and is afraid of nothing; after all, a dog that was used to hunt lions needed to be fearless.

The ridgeback is a large, reddish-brown dog with a distinctive ridge of raised hair running down its spine. In my experience, this breed is very trainable but of strong character. I have heard reports of dog trainers refusing to train them but for the life of me I don't know why.

Although ridgebacks can be stubborn and won't be bullied into anything, with the right technique they can be turned into reliable, trustworthy companions. Like any other dog, their temperament can range from submissive to determined, but in general they are a very strong-willed breed. The case history that follows tells the story of Jontty, a purebred Rhodesian ridgeback and a classic example of the breed.

Case history: I was asked to assist in the rehabilitation of Jontty by Lisa, a colleague who had been working with him. Although the obedience training had been a success, Jontty's habit of growling and jumping at anyone who approached his food was still a major concern for his owners. Lisa told me that Jontty had responded extremely well to the training and would instantly obey the voice commands and reprimands. He was the perfect dog — except when he was eating. If anyone came near him then, he turned into a fire-breathing dragon. Commands and reprimands were useless. He would stand over his food, legs spread-eagled, and would leap in the air to bite someone if they got too close.

When I arrived at the house, I went straight outside to meet Jontty. His owner began to throw Jontty's toy for him to fetch and after watching for a few minutes, I noticed something interesting. Whenever the owner tried to bend down and take the toy from Jontty, he tried to block her hand with his head, a typically possessive pose.

I asked her to wait a second and gave Jontty the command 'Leave', which I had been told was the command they'd been using to try to cure his food aggression. He looked at me with hooded eyes but still maintained his position. I growled the reprimand word 'Bah' at him and he responded immediately by spitting out the toy at his owner's feet. I praised him and asked his owner to do so too. We continued in this way for ten minutes, with his owner throwing a ball and Jontty bringing it back and dropping it on the ground when he was commanded to do so.

I felt the time was now right to try the same procedure with food, and I asked his owner to bring some out for Jontty. I have never seen a dog eat so fast! I knew I'd have to work quickly or all the food would soon be gone. I gave the command 'Leave'. When he didn't respond, I said 'Bah!' and he immediately moved away from the food. I praised him lavishly and allowed him to return to his food. I repeated this process several times until I felt sure Jontty would respond to the 'Leave' command alone.

By teaching Jontty to leave his food rather than trying to take it off him, we had a much less confrontational situation. Jontty responded to this treatment and never once tried to bite me.

Rottweilers

Rottweilers originally came from Germany. At one point they were known as 'butcher dogs', because they were used to drive the cattle to market and then to guard the farmer's

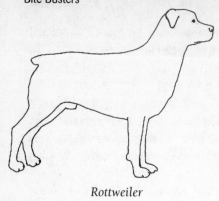

Rottweiler

money once the cattle had been sold. The farmers were also known to place a money pouch containing the day's takings around the dog's neck, confident that the dog would protect the booty while they enjoyed a well-earned ale with the other cattlemen.

The Rottweiler's ancestry is not entirely certain, but it is believed to be related to the mastiff. They are a very loyal breed, undeserving of their reputation for aggression. This reputation could be due, in part, to their formidable appearance and the fact that attacks by Rottweilers are usually well documented in the media. I have found them to be slow to anger; they would rather walk away from a confrontation than fight. They make a very trustworthy pet if trained correctly.

Rottweilers are fast becoming one of the world's most popular dogs, along with German shepherds and border collies.

Mastiffs

The mastiff is one of the oldest recognised breeds, and was originally bred as a gamekeeper's dog to help them catch poachers. Its large, flattened face and mouth enabled it to grab a poacher and hold him in its powerful jaws until the gamekeeper arrived.

The mastiff's dark mask and sober expression can make it appear unfriendly, and its size can be intimidating. I believe that the perception of these dogs as aggressive is largely due to their appearance. I have always found them to be dependable, amenable and easygoing pets.

The case history below illustrates how focused the mastiff is. It was not bred to rip flesh or maim its quarry but to apprehend and detain all intruders who dared to enter its domain.

Case history: Cathy and Ken had arranged to stay with some friends at an estate outside London. It was late at night when they arrived and the property was in darkness. Fortunately, their car lights illuminated a pillar with an intercom on it. Ken stopped the car and climbed out. He found his way through some hedges and, reaching the pillar, began to feel around for the intercom. Meanwhile, Cathy sat in the car waiting for him to return.

Ken suddenly screamed, 'Help! Something's grabbed me!' Cathy jumped out of the car and ran to his aid. She could not see or hear anything other than Ken's screams. She ran towards the sound of his voice, stumbling through the hedge, when suddenly she too was grabbed on the arm and thrown to the ground. Whatever it was now had her arm firmly in its grip. She could feel its hot breath and hear its laboured breathing. She screamed louder than she had ever screamed in her life.

Suddenly the whole area was awash with light. Someone in the house had heard their screams and had come to investigate. At last Ken and Cathy could see what it was that had silently attacked them. It was a large mastiff. Their friends prised Cathy's arms from the mastiff's jaws and took Cathy and Ken inside to investigate their injuries. Amazingly, they had no injuries at all, just a few teeth marks in their flesh.

Dobermans

Dobermans originate from the town of Apolda in Germany, where they were bred by a local magistrate named Louis Doberman. Amongst his other responsibilities, he was the keeper of the local dog pound. Using the stock he had at his disposal (its ancestors are thought to be the pinscher,

Doberman

Rottweiler, Weimeraner and Manchester terrier), he set out to breed the perfect guard dog to protect him; one that was powerfully built and remarkably strong.

The modern Doberman is a more amiable, less aggressive dog than its forebears. Extremely intelligent and often exuberant, it makes an affectionate and loyal companion. Its reputation as an excellent guard dog still stands, however; it is athletic and courageous, and quick to warn its owner of approaching strangers. This, perhaps, is why they are still perceived as aggressive, despite the fact they are rarely involved in attacks on humans.

Part 2

How to avoid being bitten

THE STAND RIGHT NO BITE TECHNIQUE

If we want to avoid an attack we need to make sure that our body language gives the dog the right message.

Many people believe that you should submit to a dog that might bite by crouching to eye level or lying on the ground. I disagree with this theory. By submitting the way a subordinate dog would, you may place yourself in extreme danger — the dog could easily bite your face and neck. There is also a popular belief that you should present a dog with the back of your hand, to allow it to sniff you. Again I feel this is a dangerous practice, especially if the dog has been hit before. A dog that has been smacked by a hand in the past might think you are going to touch it, or hit it, and could snap at you.

I've discovered that the safest way to avoid attack if approached by a growling or barking dog is to *stand totally still*. Do not attempt to pat the dog. Rather than holding out your hand, let the dog come to you. Dogs prefer to approach you on their terms. Rush them and you'll soon suffer the consequences.

When you stand still, you are imitating the behaviour of a dog that is neither submissive, nor aggressive. It is a passive pose. The dog will realise that you are not a pushover, nor are you a threat. This type of body

Do not attempt to pat the dog. Rather than holding out your hand, let the dog come to you. Dogs prefer to approach you on their own terms — rush them and you'll suffer the consequences.

29

language is the safest way to deal with all types of aggression.

I employed this technique when Brutus looked like he was going to attack me (see case history on page 6). His owner told me that he had bitten several people, one of whom had to be hospitalised.

So why did Brutus not bite me?

Unlike Brutus's other 'victims', I kept calm and stood absolutely still. I did not run and I made no quick movements. My actions were totally non-confrontational; a trick I had learned years previously when I leaned into a car window where a vicious cattle dog, unbeknown to me, was lying asleep.

I have long believed in a non-aggressive approach when it comes to warding off an attack by a dog. I call this method

If attacked, keep calm and stand totally still. When you stand still you imitate the behaviour of a dog that is neither submissive nor aggressive. It is a passive, non-confrontational pose. The dog will realise that you are not a pushover, nor are you a threat.

To reprimand the dog, say 'Bah' in a harsh voice. Do not hit the dog or try to push it away.

the Stand Right No Bite technique. My husband Danny and I developed it after many years of research and personal experiments while working with aggressive, potentially dangerous dogs.

The basics of Stand Right No Bite are as follows:

- Do not pat the dog
- Do not stare at the dog
- To reprimand the dog, say 'Bah!' in a harsh voice — never attempt to hit the dog
- If attacked, stand completely still
- Do not make any threatening or provocative movements

You should never fight back, especially if attacked by a 'fighting' dog, because you have no chance of winning and the dog could inflict serious wounds. If the dog should knock you to the ground, the safest approach is to feign death and curl up in a ball. Stay in that position until the dog loses interest.

The following case history harks back to the days when I was the chief instructor at a large dog club on the south coast of New South Wales. Many of the instructors were dog handlers from the local naval base, who'd help out at the club in their spare time. We usually agreed on most things relating to dogs, except about how best to avoid being bitten.

The naval dog handlers were adamant that the best way to deal with an attacking dog was to meet it with aggression. If they were ever attacked, they all said they would fight back. I argued that that type of approach would be disastrous. I know first-hand how hard it is to fight with a dog — they are far better equipped to fight than we are.

We always parted friends after these discussions, but invariably we begged to differ. Unfortunately, one of the instructors was soon to discover just how dangerous the 'fight back' technique actually is.

Case history: Ian's job was to help train guard dogs at the naval base. He would dress up in padded clothes and play at being the bad guy. This role was known as 'The Stirrer', and it also involved the training and agitating of all new recruit dogs. Ian loved his work and marvelled at how efficient each dog was at obeying its handler's command to attack and then bring him to ground.

One of the recent recruits, a German shepherd named Max, was proving to be a bit of a wimp. He was slow to anger and was failing Ian's attempts to make him into a good guard dog. Max just wasn't making the grade. The other handlers had even nicknamed him 'Mad Max' as a joke.

In an attempt to improve Max's performance, every day Ian would pay him special attention. As he walked past Max's enclosure, Ian would bash his baton on the gate. Max would bark for a short while, but would soon retire to his kennel, preferring not to get involved in a confrontation.

This ritual went on for some time, until one day Ian was called in to work to do kennel duty as one of the handlers was sick. The usual practice was to command the dogs to 'Kennel up', and they would obediently get into their kennels while their pens were cleaned out.

All was going well until Ian arrived at Max's enclosure. Max was involved in an altercation with the dog in the neighbouring cage and they were growling and snapping at each other through the wire. Ian entered Max's enclosure, shutting the gate behind him. He commanded Max to 'Kennel up', but Max ignored him and continued fighting with the other dog through the wire. Ian became more forceful and yelled at Max to 'Kennel up'. Max still ignored him.

Ian raised the hose he was holding and again yelled at the dog to obey. Max's expression suddenly changed. He charged at Ian, snarling and barking as he lunged. Fearing the worst, Ian turned and tried to get out of the enclosure, but the dog was on his back before he could get the gate open. He felt Max bite into his shoulder and he thrust his shoulder back in a defiant attempt to push Max away. The dog grabbed him again. Ian then turned towards the dog, trying to fend him off with his hands. Max just kept biting and biting as Ian attempted to break free, yelling at the dog to 'Leave', a command used by the handlers when they want to call off an attack. Max did not respond.

Ian's shouts had summoned his colleagues, and by this stage Ian's body was wedged against the gate and Max was on top of him. They were unable to open the gate to assist him. All the while Ian was valiantly trying to protect his face. One of the handlers grabbed a fire hose and aimed it at the dog in an attempt to get him to stop, but Max did not react. He was hell-bent on his relentless attack.

Suddenly, Ian's body went limp. He lay totally still. Max pushed him twice with his nose then retired to his kennel. At last his workmates were able to rescue Ian from the enclosure. He was badly injured and in shock.

Why did Max respond the way he did when he had seemed to be such a passive dog? Let's analyse what happened.

Over a period of time, Ian had behaved aggressively towards Max to try and make him more aggressive for the job he had to do. Instead, Max became fearful of Ian, and it is this fear that lead him to attack.

When Max charged at Ian, Ian tried to run away and escape from the pen. This behaviour told Max that Ian was frightened of him, which would have given Max more courage. When Max attacked, Ian began to fight back, and his aggression (although in self-defence) would have fuelled Max's aggression.

Once Ian went into shock and lay still, Max stopped fighting. He punched Ian twice with his nose (perhaps to see if there were any reflexes or further resistance) and then retreated to his kennel. It seems that this punching action is quite common in attack situations when the dog is confronted by someone standing or lying totally still.

In another case, again involving a German shepherd, my daughter Donna was attacked by a guard dog that leapt out of a security guard's truck when she stopped to speak to the guard. Donna had been taught from a very early age how to react if a dog attacked her. She stood stock-still. The dog punched her once with its nose, right on her stomach, then quickly withdrew to the inside of the van. She received only a small bruise. I hate to think what might have happened to her had she reacted by moving backwards as the dog launched its attack.

Although the examples I've related here both involved German shepherds, I have seen cattle dogs, Rottweilers, bull terriers, collies, Dobermans and various hunting dogs and crossbreeds punch their quarry. But not all dogs punch when confronted by a motionless victim. Some run towards the person, barking, and once close enough will sniff them then wag their tail or lose interest and wander off. Others do something much scarier — they grab the leg or arm of the person they are attacking. They don't tear the flesh, they simply stand there waiting for a reaction. These behaviours are illustrated in the next two case histories.

Case history: I was once asked to train a dog that the police had declared dangerous. It was a crossbred kelpie which had attacked and bitten five people.

The dog's owner ushered me into the house upon my arrival and expressed concern over his dog's behaviour. He then led me straight to the back door and promptly opened it, allowing me to walk through first. Suddenly, I glimpsed something black which flashed around behind me. I immediately froze. I felt the dog grab my leg and slowly turned my head to look at it.

The dog was looking up at me, waiting for a reaction. I did not move, but yelled 'Bah!' at the dog in a very harsh, guttural voice. The dog immediately let go of my leg, jumped away and stood off to one side, glaring at me with a mean glint in its eyes. I again attempted to step out the door. The dog responded immediately and grabbed my leg in its jaws, waiting for a reaction. I stood still and yelled 'Bah', and once again the dog let go. I was losing patience, so asked the owner to restrain his dog with a lead. He did, then asked if I had been bitten. I looked at my leg and there was no mark at all, not even a ladder in my stockings.

I was quite amazed by the way this dog had behaved, standing there with my leg locked in its jaws. I feel quite confidant in saying that most people in that situation would have panicked and tried to free their leg from the dog's mouth, which would almost certainly have resulted in a bite.

Up until that day, I had never been confronted by that situation, mainly because when a fear-aggressive dog runs towards me barking, I never let it get around behind me. I always stand my ground and keep turning to face the dog as it tries to go in for a rear attack. This approach tends to keep the dog circling and it has always worked for me. This type of dog seems to lack the confidence for a frontal assault. It wasn't until I heard the following story that I began to piece together this particular style of attack.

Case history: John was reading a meter at a client's house when he was attacked from behind by a bull terrier. Because he had attended my Stand Right No Bite lectures, he knew exactly what to do. He didn't move a muscle when he felt the dog grab his leg. He called out to the owner of the dog to come and help. The owner obliged then locked the dog away.

John later rang me and joked that I had just cost him $7000. I was a bit bewildered until he told me that that was the payout he'd received from the insurance company when a previous dog attack had put him in hospital.

John was saved from possible serious injury by the Stand Right No Bite technique. However, I feel the reason he had to get the owner to pull the dog away from him was because he forgot to use the word 'Bah' when the dog had hold of him. If he had, the dog might have let go in the same way as the dog that attacked me.

UNDERSTANDING A DOG'S REACTIONS

The previous section illustrates the point that dogs will have different reactions to the Stand Right No Bite technique. Understanding the reasons why individual dogs react the way they do will greatly increase your chances of staying calm in an attack situation.

Barking on approach

Just because a dog runs up to you barking does not mean it is going to attack. It barks to summon the pack (that is, its owner) and to drive off intruders. It will try to get close to you simply because it wants to sniff you.

If a dog runs up to you barking, it doesn't necessarily mean it is going to attack. It barks to summon its owner and to drive off intruders.

Punching with the nose

Based on my observations and experience, I believe dogs punch their quarry for two reasons. The first is to elicit a reaction. The dog thinks to itself, *Will this person (or dog) run away or fight?* If nothing happens, the dog retreats. The motionless response confuses it so it backs off.

The second reason is because they expect the victim to either run or fight back. If the victim does not move, the dog actually collides with them.

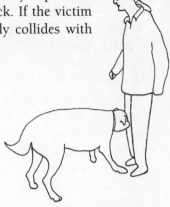

If you stand completely still when attacked, the dog may punch you with its nose to try to elicit a reaction. Your motionless response will confuse it, and the dog will retreat.

Case history: Todd was a meter reader who had been attacked by a cattle dog in the course of his work. It had bitten him several times on the back of his legs and buttocks as he tried to escape and he had spent several days in hospital as a result.

The attack had so traumatised Todd that he was unable to do his job properly. Whenever he came to a house with a dog in the yard, he would pass it by. His employers were concerned about his lack of productivity, though they were not unsympathetic to his plight. Many other employees had had terrifying experiences with dogs which had affected their ability to carry out their work. Deciding to take positive action, the electricity company contacted Bark Busters and arranged for us to instruct their staff in the Stand Right No Bite technique.

After attending the lectures, Todd felt a lot more confident about coming into contact with strange dogs. It was not long before the opportunity arose to put his new knowledge to the test. He was called out to a block of units, where he noticed a sign on the building that said 'Guard dog on premises'. Todd assumed that the dog – if there was one – would be locked inside one of the units.

As he was reading the meter, he heard a bark and what sounded like a large dog running down the stairs towards him.

His first thought was to run, but the exit was too far away. Suddenly the dog appeared and launched itself at him. He was terrified.

At that instant, Todd remembered all the things I had said in my lecture. Thinking his chances of escaping alive were pretty slim, he decided he may as well try what he had been trained to do. He stood totally still, clasped his hands in front of him and braced himself for the attack. At the moment of impact he was holding his breath, almost as if he were afraid to breathe.

The dog, a large German shepherd, punched him twice with its nose then retreated back up the stairs. Todd relaxed and sighed with relief. The dog had not bitten him! Todd was able to see, first-hand, how effective the Stand Right No Bite technique is, and to this day has not been bitten by another dog.

Holding with the mouth

Rather than biting, some dogs will grab hold of the person's leg. This, I believe, is because the dog is attempting to repel the intruder. However, when it is confronted with someone who doesn't move, the dog becomes confused and just stands there waiting for them to react.

It seems that certain breeds, such as cattle dogs, kelpies and sheepdogs, are more likely to behave this way, as they employ this technique to round up sheep and cattle. It is also a trait of fear-aggressive dogs which lack the courage for a frontal attack.

A fear-aggressive dog often lacks the courage for a frontal attack. Instead, it will attack from behind, and may grab your leg. If you stand still it will become confused and, rather than biting you, will just hold your leg in its mouth. If you shout 'Bah' in a harsh voice, the dog will usually let go.

Knocking to the ground

When under attack, the victim is invariably frightened, and may trip over and fall to the ground when trying to escape. However, sometimes a dog will actually knock the person over in an attempt to dominate them. It will rear up, trying to gain the advantage. Once it has the person on the ground, it will try to keep them there, biting at their face and neck in order to make them submit.

I read about a man in England who was attacked by two pit bull terriers on his way home from work. The man's face was savagely mauled and his nose and part of his ears were bitten off in the frenzy. One of the things he said in the interview was that he felt he was fighting for his life. This is because he was fighting dogs that were bred

An attacking dog may knock you over in an attempt to dominate you. Do not attempt to hit the dog, but cover your face with your arms and keep still. The more you struggle, the more aggressive the dog will become.

to attack relentlessly. The more he struggled and tried to get up on his feet, the more the dogs would have tried to make him submit, all the while inflicting horrendous injuries to the poor man's face and arms.

A dog of comparable size to the attackers in the same situation would have fared much better than the human victim. Dogs are far more capable of withstanding an attack of this ferocity. They are covered in fur and their skin stretches rather than rips. Most attacks on other dogs focus on the neck and ears, as it prevents the victim from biting its aggressor. When a dog attacks an adult, however, the majority of bites are on the legs, arms and buttocks. This is obviously because of our size in comparison to the dog. With children, the bites are normally on the face or around the head. (See 'Dog-proofing children' on page 71.) Of course, if an adult is knocked to the ground they, too, are at greater risk of injury to the face and neck.

The best thing to do in this situation is to roll into a ball, cover your face with your arms and remain completely still.

A DOG'S SENSES

Dogs have the same five senses we have — sight, hearing, smell, taste and touch. Although their vision is inferior to ours, they are able to hear and smell far better than we can. Understanding a dog's senses is one of the keys to avoiding an attack, and the two most important of these are *smell* and *sight*.

Smell

A dog's sense of smell is extremely acute. That is why they are used to detect drugs that have been smuggled at the airport and to track down people who are lost in the bush. They are able to distinguish scents that might be days old and accurately follow the path someone has walked days earlier.

However, a dog has to come very close to something to scent it. So even though the dog's sense of smell is greater than ours, like ours it has its limitations. To scent and analyse a track where a human has walked, the dog has to put its nose close to the ground. The only time it doesn't is when there is a breeze blowing the scent towards the dog, which enables it to 'air scent'.

While at the RSPCA, I rescued a blind miniature silky terrier from a very busy street. I called her Mini and I cared for her while we tried to find her owners. During the weeks I had her, we grew very fond of each other.

During working hours, I kept her in a cage out the back until it was time to go home. Each afternoon one of the staff would bring her into the office and place her on the ground. She would immediately start sniffing around for me. I watched her closely as she sniffed each person in turn, in an attempt to find me. I noticed that she had to get very close to each person to sniff them. It wasn't until she found me that she would get excited and wriggle her whole body. Her nose had told her she had found her friend.

So, when a dog sees you on its property, be aware that it has to get very close to scent who or what it is. This is why some dogs will run up to you barking, then sniff you. Many people panic in a situation like this, which increases the likelihood of an attack. If you stand still, the dog will most probably sniff you and then walk away.

Sight

There is much debate about how well dogs see. Scientists have found the dog's eye to be lacking in some components of the human eye. I have spoken to many vets and dog experts, as well as conducting my own experiments, and the consensus is that a dog's vision is comparable to that of a person wearing glasses which are not designed for their eyes. They have reasonably good binocular vision and can detect the slightest sign of movement. They can distinguish shapes, but do not recognise faces, and it is thought they see in black and white and shades of grey.

The German police force conducted a test some years ago which demonstrated the limitations of a dog's eyesight. The test was conducted indoors, where there was no chance of a breeze aiding the dog's sense of smell. They seated the police dog handlers in a row at one end of the room, then brought in a dog and allowed the handler to call to it. The dog reacted immediately and went straight to its handler.

They then took the dog out of the room, shuffled the seating arrangements and then let the dog back in the room. The dog first ran straight to the same spot where its handler had been sitting and sniffed the person there. Realising that he was not its handler, the dog then sniffed each person in turn until it found its handler.

The reaction was the same no matter which dog they used or what the handler was wearing. None of the dogs could recognise the facial features of its handler.

My own tests bear this out. No matter how close I get to my dogs or other dogs that I have used in the tests, not one has yet been able to recognise its owner by the way they look. The dog recognises them by the way they walk, their voice, the area or car they alighted from and their scent.

I first discovered the limitations of a dog's sight and its scenting powers several years ago when I stepped out onto my back verandah with a white towel wrapped around my head. I heard growling and looked up to see my German shepherd Monty, who was lying on the grass, staring at me. I couldn't believe he didn't recognise me. I was staring right at him and was only about 3 metres away, yet he showed no signs of recognition.

I decided to play along and see how far I could go. I crouched down and took a step towards him. He became more agitated and his growl grew in intensity. I could see him trying to sniff the air, but the breeze was blowing in my face and he couldn't smell me.

I kept edging closer. Suddenly, he leapt to his feet and barked at me. He had no idea what this creature was, but I could tell he wanted to scare it away. When the bark didn't work, he ran at me and I stood still. He was about a metre away and was now barking and circling, unsure what to do next. He kept glancing towards the house, obviously wondering why I had not come out to see what was happening.

I stood there waiting for him to recognise me. Still he kept growling and circling. Finally he moved closer and sniffed my leg. I could see his body stance change immediately. His ears went back, his head dropped and he wiggled his body from side to side as he whined and licked my hands.

INTERPRETING A DOG'S BODY LANGUAGE

Dogs may not be able to talk, but their actions speak a thousand words. Their tail, ears, mouth, eyes and stance telegraph many things to the trained observer. The ability to interpret a dog's body language plays a very big part in being able to recognise an impending attack. By learning each of the signs discussed below, you will have a much better chance of avoiding an attack — no matter what the situation.

Tail

Many people believe that a wagging tail is the sign of a friendly dog. However, I have seen many guard dogs and hunting dogs wagging their tails vigorously just before they were unleashed to attack.

A wagging tail simply means the dog is anticipating something. It could be any number of things: a meal, a pat, a game, a pending attack, or waiting for a cat to climb down from a tree.

A wagging tail alone is not sufficient to prove a dog is safe and friendly. You need to look for positive signs in other aspects of its body language before you can be sure.

A tail held up over the dog's back in an erect position is the sign of a dominant dog. The dog may also increase its height by stretching up on its toes and walking with stiff legs. This position also indicates an aggressive dog. A submissive dog will usually keep its tail down or stuck firmly between its legs. Apart from the fact that this prevents other dogs from sniffing its bottom, it is also a signal to those dogs that it does not pose a threat. In comparison, a friendly dog will usually hold its tail straight out and level with its body, and it will wag its tail in that position.

Even a dog that has a tail which curls over its back, such as the husky or Samoyed, still reacts with its tail depending on its temperament and the situation.

The tail is one of the main indications of a dog's mood, and it can say much about what the animal is thinking or what it intends to do in a given situation, but an accurate assessment depends on the body language as a whole.

Ears

Because a dog constantly moves its ears to pick up sounds, it can be difficult to interpret the underlying meaning of a particular position. For instance, if the ears are lying backwards or flat against the head, it generally depicts friendliness or acceptance, but unless this gesture is accompanied by other positive signs, it is not a definite indication of amiability. It could indicate a fearful dog, which is displaying submissive tendencies to let you know that it is not a threat and is not dominant enough to challenge you. It does not necessarily mean you can pat the dog or that it accepts you. The dog might be quite okay if you don't try to pat it, but might snap at you if you do.

Pricked ears can indicate a dominant, aggressive dog, or a confident dog that is interested in what you are doing. However, it is not a definite sign that the dog is likely to attack.

Always keep in mind the golden rule: never pat a dog until it fully accepts you (see 'Approaching a dog' on page 51).

Mouth

A dog uses its mouth in much the same way we use our hands. If it is itchy in a place that is out of reach of its back legs, it will bite the area with its mouth. If a fly annoys it, it will snap at the fly and try to catch it. If its leg is trapped, it will bite at whatever entraps it in an attempt to break free. If it is cornered and frightened, it will try to fight its way out by snapping and biting.

In addition to these things, the mouth also relays exactly how the dog is feeling. A relaxed, panting mouth is a definite sign that the dog is not concerned about you. A tight-lipped mouth, on the other hand, indicates that the dog is worried. Do the wrong thing and it could bite you.

A closed mouth takes on a different meaning if the dog's tongue is poking in and out as you approach. The protruding tongue is a sign of submission, but this dog has to be treated very gently and must not be rushed. It is feeling apprehensive and is subliminally letting you know.

Any form of licking is always a submissive act and any form of biting is a dominant act, even in very young puppies that play-bite.

A fearful dog will usually bare its teeth. The more teeth you see, the more fearful the dog. A closed mouth usually indicates a less fearful dog, but this largely depends on the circumstances. For instance, a dog that growls with its mouth closed while you are patting or examining it is afraid that you will hurt it, perhaps because it has been hurt in a similar situation in the past. A dog that growls at you with its mouth closed when you enter its domain, is warning you that it is in charge — tread carefully.

Never pat a growling dog. If you do, you're asking for trouble. You don't know the dog's history — perhaps it has been mistreated. The following story about a dog my husband Danny treated for aggression demonstrates why you should never pat a strange dog, let alone a growling one.

> **Case history:** Danny was called in to treat an extremely over-active cattle dog with a barking and aggression problem. During his visit the owners showed him how the dog reacted if they attempted to pat her.
>
> Danny asked them if they had ever hit the dog and they said they had, in an effort to stop her barking. Danny pointed out that that is why the dog was growling at them. She was afraid of what they were going to do to her and she no longer trusted them. Danny very quickly turned the problem around by getting them to feed the dog every time they patted her, and showed them how to stop the barking using a more humane technique.

Eyes

A dog says a lot with its eyes. After many years observing dogs, I am now able to judge their temperament by looking at their eyes.

A dog lacking confidence will lower its head and look up at you with hooded eyes. Only the bottom half of the eye will be visible, and quite a lot of white will show below the iris. A fearful dog will have wide open, staring eyes, which will dart about in all directions. A dominant dog will stare at you, and will approach you from the front.

A confident, friendly dog will appear to have smiling eyes. Its eyes will be neither hooded nor wide open, and there will be little or no white visible.

When you piece together all the signals a dog conveys through body language, you have a complete picture of how the dog feels about you. This information will help you to determine whether or not you are in danger of being attacked.

The easiest way for a relative beginner to understand and

act on this information is to remember the following:

- A dog that walks stiffly, possibly on its toes, with very definite movements, ears forward, tail erect, eyes staring at your face and hackles up, should always be regarded with respect. Stand totally still, plant your feet slightly apart and do not pat the dog. Allow the dog to sniff

A dominant dog

and assess you. You should at all times remain on the spot and only turn as the dog does. Wait for the dog to lose interest in you. Bit by bit, move towards your car or the gate, but never take your eyes off the dog.

- A dog that runs towards you barking with its tail in the air and hackles up, but as it gets closer puts its tail between its legs and attempts to get behind you, is a frightened dog. It is afraid to attack you from the front. Try to face the dog at all times. Turn as the dog circles you, and stand totally still if it darts at your legs or attempts to attack you. Always keep your eye on the dog and try to keep you back against a wall or a car. Use your voice aggressively; yell 'Bah!' Do not use jerky actions.

A submissive dog

- A dog that totally submits to you, rolling over on its back or crouching down with its ears back and tail between its legs, should not be patted. Under no

47

circumstances pat a strange dog until it shows you clear acceptance. (See 'Approaching a dog' on page 51.)

• A friendly dog will show no signs of tension or fear. It will lower its head, lick its lips or pant. Its tail is more likely to be in a straight line, level with its body rather than erect, or between its legs. An extremely friendly dog will look like it's smiling

A friendly dog

and will usually wag its whole body as it wags its tail.

CONTROLLING YOUR REACTIONS

Our reflexes are involuntary responses, in part designed to help us avoid serious injury. If we didn't have reflexes we wouldn't quickly pull our hand away from a hot stove when we accidentally touched it or put our hands up to protect ourselves when something came flying towards our head. When it comes to an attack by a dog, however, our reflexes can get us bitten. I discovered this quite by accident when I was chief instructor of a country dog training club, though it took me a few years to understand why.

I had raced over to my friend's car to tell her something before she left the training ground. I had heard stories about her dog King, a very aggressive cattle dog that asked no questions if a human invaded his domain. As I leaned on the window of the car to speak to my friend, I noticed a blue flash rocketing towards me. It was King. I knew I had no chance of avoiding the attack; instinct told me to stay put.

He was upon me in no time. He punched my arm with his nose but because I did not move a muscle he withdrew, giving me a look that seemed to say, What is that? It doesn't appear to be human. My friend looked at me in amazement. She was sure I had been bitten. I looked at my arm and there was no damage at all. My thin blouse had a small amount of saliva on it, but that was it.

As the years passed, I applied the same technique many, many times but it wasn't until I managed an RSPCA shelter that I understood why it worked.

One of the tasks I hated at the RSPCA was dealing with wild cats. We would sometimes have to use catching poles to move them from the traps to a cage and to recapture them when they escaped. I started to notice certain things about the way the cats behaved towards the catching poles compared with the way they reacted when a human handled them. They would grab the catching pole, but would soon let go. At first I thought it was because the poles were made of wood, but their reaction to rubber was the same. Then it occurred to me: did the cats let go because inanimate objects don't have reflexes? Perhaps if I did not react when attacked my injuries would be reduced.

It wasn't long before I was able to put my theory to the test. I was trying to sedate a large cream Persian that had a mean streak, and it grabbed me as it broke free from the grasp of my assistant, Michael. It wrapped its claws around my arm and sunk its teeth into my hand. Consciously, I held my arm still and did not move. The cat seemed to be mesmerised. It stopped moving and, although it still had my hand in its mouth, it was not biting any deeper. It was as if the world had stood still. Suddenly, I asked Michael to get the cat off my hand. He seemed as if he, too, had been in a trance, but he snapped out of it immediately and began prising the cat from my hand. My injuries were minimal and my tetanus shots were up-to-date, so I was not concerned. I still have the scar today but it is pretty insignificant. I am sure it would have been a much more serious wound if I had struggled and tried to pull away from the cat.

FEARFUL PERSON – FEARFUL DOG

One of the most explosive situations with regard to a potential dog attack is when a person who is frightened of dogs meets a dog that is frightened of people. This combination is a dangerous cocktail that could result in a serious attack.

When I popped into a video store recently to return some tapes, there was a large female Rottweiler waiting for her owners outside the entrance to the store. I was in a hurry and I brushed past the dog, which received a bit of a shock and jumped. I faced her and stood still, allowing her to sniff and assess me, after which she appeared to settle. I moved off, keeping my eye on her, knowing that a fearful dog might try to give me a sneaky bite as I walked away if I were to inadvertently take my eyes off it.

That could very easily have turned into a bite situation if I had been someone who was afraid of dogs and had reacted adversely — the way my cleaner did the first time she met my two lovable dogs. They had approached her the way they approach everyone — they rushed up to her confidently, looking for a pat. She reacted with fear, the same way the Rottweiler reacted when I entered the video shop. She jumped about, holding her hands in the air and moving away from them every time they got close enough to sniff her. The dogs seemed to be thinking *Who is this strange creature? Why is she reacting this way?* They were so used to being around dog-lovers that they just didn't know quite how to deal with this behaviour.

Imagine if my cleaner had met the Rottweiler. That could have been a disaster.

If you are frightened of dogs, the best thing to do is stand still and allow the dog to sniff you. Do not make any sudden movements and try not to show your fear. It is not necessary to pat or make friends with it if you don't feel comfortable.

APPROACHING A DOG

All dogs must be approached with care. Never assume a dog will not bite. Always wait for it to accept you first. Allow it to sniff you, until it loses interest and wanders off. Then, and only then, should you move. If in doubt, do not approach the dog at all. Rushing up to an adorable-looking dog is definitely not the correct approach.

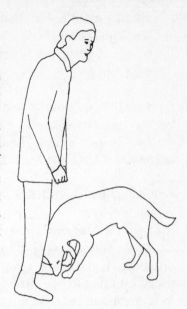

To be able to scent and assess you, a dog needs to come very close. Do not move until the dog has lost interest — the dog must accept you first, not the other way round.

Case history: Patrick worked as a field officer for the Australian Electoral Commission and his job involved collecting cards from people who were registering to vote. One day, accompanied by a fellow officer, Mike, he called at a house where there were two large golden retrievers. Patrick immediately tried to make friends with them, but Mike ignored the dogs, telling Patrick to leave them alone. Patrick disregarded the warning and patted and played with the two dogs while Mike collected the enrolment card.

Mike headed for the gate. Patrick stopped playing with the dogs and, turning his back on them, went to leave. Suddenly one of the dogs reared up, grabbing him from behind, and thrust its paws into the pockets of his jacket, making it impossible for him to get away.

Patrick called to his friend for help, but Mike was too busy laughing to be able to do anything. Patrick was trapped; he had no way of getting free without his friend's help. He was at the dog's mercy.

Patrick's dilemma shows that there is more than one reason why it's not a good idea to make friends with a strange dog. In the situation above, the dog could have easily become aggressive when Patrick tried to free himself from its grasp.

APPROACHING A VICIOUS DOG

Many of the case histories I've related so far have described situations where people did not realise that the dog would bite them. If you know a dog is vicious and likely to attack, the safest thing to do is *avoid confrontation*. If, however, you have no option but to confront it, then take some food with you. Many dogs will sell their soul for a scrap of food, and it will help win the dog over. (See page 63.)

If circumstances get out of hand, adopt the Stand Right No Bite technique described on page 29.

Case history: Jason worked for a promotions company delivering leaflets door-to-door. With three German shepherds of his own, Jason had no fear of dogs and loved his work.

One day he approached a house without fences. 'Be careful,' a voice called out. 'They have a vicious dog and it always attacks people who try to put things in that letterbox.' It was the voice of a woman in the adjoining yard.

Jason felt he could cope with any dog, regardless of how big or scary it was. He opened the letterbox. Nothing could have prepared him for what he was about to see. He heard a rustle in the bushes, followed by an enormous growl and ferocious bark. He looked up. Coming straight towards him was the biggest dog he'd ever seen.

The dog was a large black Great Dane, and from the look on its face, Jason knew it wasn't friendly. He decided that he had to get out of there as fast as he could. He glanced around quickly, and the only thing close by was a big oak tree. He decided that was his only chance of escape.

Moving extremely quickly, he made one mighty leap, grabbed the highest branch he could, and clambered up the tree. The dog stood on its hind legs with its front paws resting on the tree. It was looking straight up at Jason, snapping and snarling and sounding extremely frustrated.

'Are you okay?' the neighbour called out from the safety of her own yard, in a rather concerned voice.

'Yes,' Jason replied, 'but I don't know how I can get down now I am up here.'

Then he had a thought. 'Do you have some diced chicken or a doggy treat in your house?' he inquired.

'Just a minute,' the woman said. She raced inside, returning a few minutes later with some diced chicken in a dish. 'Is this what you wanted?'

'That's fine,' replied Jason. 'Just throw some over the fence to the dog.'

The woman looked concerned. 'This is a very low fence. I'm afraid it might jump over and attack me.'

'Look, I think it's the letterbox that sets the dog off. It doesn't appear to be responding to you or anyone who passes. I honestly don't believe it will go for you at all. Could you please try feeding it? If you can just distract it for a minute, I'm sure I could climb down and get away.'

The woman called to the dog, but it stood up and growled at Jason. She called out again and this time threw some chicken to it. The dog appeared to falter, then slowly trotted towards the food, which it sniffed then ate. It was now very interested in the woman, wagging its tail and looking for more.

Jason began edging his way down the tree, keeping one eye on the dog and one on where he was putting his feet. Slowly and carefully he climbed from branch to branch until it was only a short jump to the ground.

He called out to the woman again. 'Could you throw the next piece of food right down the side of the house so I can make it to your fence?'

She responded immediately by throwing the food way down the side of the house. Jason had to act quickly. He thrust his body forward and down, landing so heavily he nearly fell over. Keeping one eye on the dog, he ran towards the fence.

The dog had now finished eating and as soon as it saw Jason it barked and chased after him. Jason threw himself at the fence and bolted over it, landing on his back.

He was free.

When Jason related this story to me, he asked me what I would have done in the same situation. I told him that I would not have fled: I would have stood my ground and allowed the dog to assess me, regardless of how scary it looked. But I could not condemn his response that day — under pressure he'd had to arrive at a quick solution to a serious problem.

If you know you can jump over a fence, climb a tree or hop into a nearby car, then go for it. *But you must be sure that you can make it to safety, otherwise running will only encourage the dog to attack you.*

I went on to tell Jason that in view of what he'd told me about the dog's reaction to food when the neighbour fed it, I strongly believe that if he had been carrying some food, the dog would have reacted to him in the same way.

COPING WITH MORE THAN ONE DOG

If you are attacked by more than one dog, the Stand Right No Bite technique still applies. Stand completely still; do not move a muscle. If you are able to, stand with your back to a wall or car. This will prevent one of the dogs attacking you from behind. If you have any food (dog kibble or dog biscuits are best), you could try feeding the dogs. Throw the food on the ground and, once the dogs have eaten it, keep throwing more food further and further away from you until the dogs are far enough from you to enable you to escape safely. And remember, always keep an eye on what the dogs are doing, but never stare at them.

The Stand Right No Bite technique applies even when there is more than one dog. Stand completely still, ideally with your back to a wall to stop the dogs attacking you from behind. If you have any food, throw it on the ground and keep throwing it further and further away from you until you are able to escape.

AGGRESSION WHEN THE OWNER IS PRESENT

When a dog enters a new home, it does not look upon its owner as a different species but as another dog. It sees itself as part of a pack whether there is only one owner or a whole family. As time passes, it starts to work out where it fits in the pecking order.

It stands to reason that a potential biter will be far more confident when it's with its owner than when it is on its own. My dog Bullseye is the most docile creature you could ever meet, but even he became aggressive one day when he stumbled upon me trying on a hat and did not recognise me.

55

He stood about 2 metres away, growling at me with hackles raised. My husband, hearing the noise, ran up the stairs to see what Bullseye was growling at. As Danny approached, Bullseye ran at me. It was clear that the thought of being backed up by the 'boss' gave him the confidence to launch an attack upon the monster in his home.

A dog is more confident and therefore more likely to attack when its owner is present. If you come across an owner and their dog in the course of your work, always ask the owner to lock up their pet.

(By the way, when Bullseye ran at me, I simply said his name and he stopped and sniffed me, then wagged his tail in recognition.)

In my lectures, I always tell the class that if they come across an owner *and* a dog when entering properties, they should *always* ask the owner to lock up the dog. The following case history is about a man who failed to do this and was attacked as a result.

Case history: Dean was a meter reader for an electricity company, and while out doing his rounds he came to a property with a German shepherd in the yard. He had been there many times before and although the dog would bark continuously, it had never come near him. Dean would safely enter the yard and leave without incident.

However, on this particular occasion, the owner was in the yard with the dog. Dean stopped at the gate and, remembering what I had taught him, asked the owner to lock up the dog. The owner replied, 'What for? The dog has never attacked you before, so why should I put him away now?'

Not wanting to get into an argument, Dean relented. Everything appeared to be fine. The dog kept its distance as Dean read the meter then walked towards the gate. The dog's owner opened the gate for him and bid him farewell. But as he stepped through the gate, Dean felt a searing pain on the back of his leg. The dog had grabbed his thigh and was pulling him to the ground.

Dean had to be taken to hospital and, as a result of his injuries, spent three months off work. All this could have been avoided if Dean had insisted that the owner lock up his dog.

A dog can also be incited to attack if its owner is yelling at you. I remember an attack in Queensland that resulted in several people being admitted to hospital. The owner of the dog was going on a fishing trip with some of his friends, and when he spotted them waiting for him beside the boat, he jokingly shouted, 'Hey! Get away from that boat!' The dog, picking up on the tone of his owner's voice, ran at the men, scattering them in all directions and snapping and biting them as they tried to escape. The owner later told me that the more he yelled at the dog to stop, the more aggressive it became towards the other men. In the end, he had to grab hold of its collar and drag his pet off his friends.

STARING: A PROVOCATIVE ACT

In Part 1, I mentioned that dogs are descended from wolves, and many of their traits are inherited from their ancestors. Researchers have found that if a subordinate wolf is stared at by the pack leader, it will avert its eyes. If the subordinate wolf is silly enough to stare back, a fight ensues.

Similarly, staring is considered to be a very provocative act in the dog world. It amounts to a challenge. A vet once told me that whenever he has to examine a dog's eyes, he always muzzles the animal in case it bites him. He firmly believes my theory that staring can incite a dog to attack.

Case history: I was called in to treat a German shepherd named Razor which had attacked several people. His owners lived on a large, sprawling property in the country and Razor had the run of the place. Most of his victims were bitten when they attempted to enter the property.

When I arrived, I was met by a very large, vicious black German shepherd. He charged at me several times, and each time I stood my ground and faced him, keeping my eye on him but not staring.

Eventually the owners heard the commotion and came out to see what was happening. They restrained Razor and we

By staring at a dog, you are challenging it to attack.

all went into the house. Once inside, Razor was fine. I explained to his owners how they should deal with his aggression and showed them how to ensure it did not happen again.

Two hours later, we were proceeding well with the training when the phone rang. It was bad news. Razor had bitten someone that morning and he was now in hospital.

The man had come to do some general repairs, and when he had entered the grounds, Razor ran at him, barking. The man decided to use a technique that had always worked for him in the past. He believed that staring at a dog would make it run away or stop it attacking, so he stared intently at Razor. Unfortunately, this only made Razor more ferocious, and the man was badly injured as a result of Razor's vicious attack.

The dog's owners asked me how I had been able to avoid attack, so I explained my system and gave them a demonstration. By now Razor had fully accepted me and was displaying no aggression at all. He was lying under a tree, panting and watching us as we spoke. I told his owners to watch carefully and I began staring at the dog. He instantly jumped up and ran at me, hackles up and growling. I immediately averted my eyes and he stopped in his tracks and returned to lie under the tree.

The subject of staring at dogs always comes up in the course of my Stand Right No Bite lectures. Recently, one of the attendees asked me why dogs don't seem to like him. He told me that he can be on a property with one of his workmates and the dog will ignore them and attack him.

I asked him if he was frightened of dogs and he said he was. I asked if he stared at them, and he said he did. I explained to him that is why the dogs always go for him rather than his colleagues, because by staring at a dog he is challenging it to attack.

KEEPING YOUR EYE ON THE DOG

Keeping your eye on the dog must not be confused with staring at it. The two are very different. Because humans have peripheral vision, we are able to see what is going on around us without looking at it directly. When you are driving a car, for example, you will notice another car in the lane beside you even though you are staring at the road ahead.

When entering a yard or property where there is a dog, make sure you know what the dog is doing. A frightened dog will always attack from behind. You have a better chance of avoiding such an attack if you keep an eye on the dog and don't turn your back on it.

Do not kick, hit or push a dog, no matter what the circumstances are — it could encourage an attack. The correct approach is to stand completely still, and make no provocative movements. Vocally reprimand the animal by saying 'Bah' in a harsh voice.

DO NOT BE AGGRESSIVE

Another golden rule for avoiding a dog attack is never be aggressive towards the dog in any physical way; do not kick or push it away with your hands. But that doesn't mean you can't yell at the dog. Shouting 'Bah' in a harsh voice will often stop a dog in its tracks.

The case history on page 8, which tells the story of David and the bull terrier, clearly shows how aggression can spell trouble. All it does is encourage further aggression from the confident or dominant dog, and may even provoke an attack from a fearful dog.

The following story is about a postal worker who was delivering more than the mail and how his aggressive behaviour towards a dog landed him in hospital.

Case history: While on his mail rounds, Jim had a habit of flicking dogs on the nose with a rubber band. Every dog that barked at him through a fence received the same treatment. Jim enjoyed his barbaric game — that is, until the day he did it to Casey, a year-old blue cattle dog.

Casey was not by nature a savage dog; in fact, she was a very lovable pet and enjoyed greeting people with a friendly bark as they approached her house. Casey's owner had been taking her to the local dog club for obedience training for several months and the people there loved her. She would always run up to everyone she saw and jump all over them, looking for a pat.

Casey would not have known what hit her when Jim flicked her with a rubber band. It certainly did not stop her barking at the gate, instead she became aggressive. Her owner was so concerned about how her lovable dog was behaving that she called me in to cure her aggression.

Before I was able to attend to the problem, however, I received a call from Casey's owner. She was distraught. She told me that she had been clearing some rubbish from her garden and had inadvertently left the gate open. Casey had obviously heard Jim's whistle and thought it was her chance to get her own back. She rushed out the gate and attacked him. Her owner could not believe this was her lovable little pet behaving so out of character.

Jim tried frantically to avoid being bitten. He kicked out at the dog with his boots, but no matter how hard he kicked her in the face and chest, Casey just came back for more. Meanwhile, Jim's bike was going everywhere. He had stopped concentrating on where he was going and was focusing only on the dog. He drove straight out into the middle of the road and into the path of a car.

Jim was taken to hospital with a fractured collar bone, lacerations and some bites to the legs. Casey was reported as a savage dog and her owner was awaiting word from the police as to Casey's fate.

Casey's story clearly shows how aggression can breed aggression and how a person who thinks they're safe because a dog is behind a fence can come unstuck. Not all postal workers are like Jim, of course. I know of one in Sydney who has a much better idea of how to soothe the savage beast. He carries a bag of dry dog food with him and feeds every dog on his round. If a dog isn't there, he leaves a little food in the letterbox! The dogs are happy because they get fed, the owners are happy because their dogs love the postie, and he is happy because the dogs are pleased to see him.

DEALING WITH A FENCE-JUMPER

If a dog jumps the fence as you walk past, it can be very frightening. It may seem that the dog is going to great lengths to get at you, but it does not mean that the dog is a vicious monster. In reality, it is no different from any other potential attack situation — you should always follow the Stand Right No Bite procedure.

CORNERED DOGS

When a fear-aggressive dog is cornered, it is much more likely to attack than at any other time. It feels threatened, and because it is unable to escape, it may believe it has no option but to fight. There are many situations in which dogs might feel cornered. The most common are when a dog is:

• On a chain
• In an enclosure
• Backed into a corner or up against a wall
• In its kennel
• In a car
• In a room
• In a small yard

The story about Ian and the German shepherd Max (see page 32), as well as pointing out how dangerous aggression towards a dog can be, illustrates how a dog is more likely to attack when it feels trapped. The following case history shows how a cornered dog which is behaving aggressively can act totally differently once the problem is alleviated. I have had dogs try to bite me as I tried to take hold of their collar when they were in a cage or kennel. Yet once I coaxed them out, I was able to take hold of their collar without so much as a growl.

Case history: When my daughter Donna was working at a boarding kennel during school holidays, she rang asking for my help to get a dog back into its kennel. The dog was frightened, and had escaped into the outer enclosure when my daughter entered the kennel to feed it. It had avoided all her attempts to recapture it by sitting in a corner and snapping at her each time she tried to grab its collar.

When I arrived, I asked Donna to fetch me some food for the dog. I figured it must be hungry as it had not yet had its meal. I approached the dog with the dish in my hand and crouched down. I stretched out my hand so that the dish was in front of the dog, and allowed it to sniff the food. I then moved the dish to my left, forcing the dog to stretch to reach it. As the dog moved forward to get the food, I moved a little closer to the corner. I repeated this manoeuvre until the dog was no longer in the corner – I was. I then placed the food on the ground. I was now behind it and took hold of its collar as it happily ate the food, no longer worried about me.

(**Note:** Crouching when dealing with fearful dogs is potentially dangerous. This technique should only be used in certain circumstances by those who know what they are doing. If you were to crouch down to a strange dog, you could be attacked. See page 66, 'Maintain your height advantage.')

USING FOOD TO STOP AGGRESSION

There is a well-known saying that food soothes the savage beast. This is true, but only when used appropriately. When dealing with aggressive dogs, food should be used either to distract them (as I did with Carlo — see page 68) or to help them overcome their fear of strangers. It should *never* be used to reward aggression.

In other words, if a dog is frightened of strangers and tries to attack when you approach, feeding it may curb its aggression. Rather than concentrating on you, the dog may focus on the food and, in future, associate a stranger with food rather than fear. However, if the dog was given food by the owner immediately after it was aggressive towards you, it could encourage the aggression. The dog could associate aggression towards strangers with a reward.

Early this century, Pavlov, a Russian physiologist and physician experimenting with animal behaviour, discovered that dogs learn by association. By ringing a bell at the same time as the dogs were fed, Pavlov was eventually able to get the dogs to salivate at the sound of the bell — associating the bell with food. Using the same principle, it stands to reason that if a dog learns that strangers are a source of food, it is more likely to be friendly towards them than frightened and aggressive.

If you feel you're at risk of an attack, perhaps because your job involves entering other people's properties or your neighbour's dog seems aggressive, it is advisable to carry non-perishable dog food with you at all times. That way, if

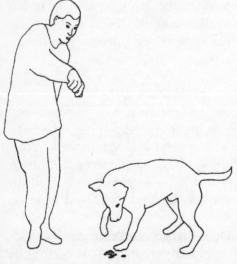

Food can be used to distract an aggressive dog. It can also help the dog overcome its fear of you. Speak in a soft voice and throw a handful of dry dog food on the ground, but do not try to pat the dog.

you get into a sticky situation, the food might just be your ticket out.

> **Case history:** A meter reader from Newcastle was able to avoid what could have been a serious attack by a pit bull terrier by using food as a diversion. In the course of her work, she had entered a property and was confronted by an aggressive dog. Her first thought was to run, but she did not like her chances of getting out of the yard without serious injury. Then she remembered the dog food in her pocket, which she had purchased after attending one of my lectures. She reached into her pocket and threw a handful on the ground. The dog immediately ceased its aggressive behaviour and gobbled up the food.
>
> The woman continued throwing food on the ground, a little further away from her each time, and carefully edged her way to the gate. She avoided any quick movements which could incite the dog to attack, knowing the time would come when she would run out of food.
>
> When she reached the gate, she threw some food behind the dog. As soon as it turned around, she was out the gate in a flash, closing it behind her.

STOPPING YOUR OWN DOG BITING YOU

Avoid provocative actions

Many people are bitten by their own dog or a dog they know well because their approach or the way they discipline the dog is far too provocative. Pointing at a dog, bending over a dog, grabbing a dog by the scruff of its neck and hitting a dog are all provocative actions which could lead to an attack.

Of the attacks on owners that I have investigated, about 85 per cent are the result of many months of physical discipline. Over a period of time, the dog starts to become conditioned to the fact that if it hears its owner's voice raised in anger, it will very shortly be followed by an aggressive act from the owner. Rather than just waiting to be hit, the dog reacts with aggression as soon as its owner starts to verbally abuse it.

Case history: Jewel was a magnificent Siberian husky, so named because of his beautiful blue eyes. Because he wanted to have a well-behaved dog, as soon as Jewel was old enough his owner had taken him to a local obedience school.

Jewel's training progressed well, until he was about eight months old – the doggy version of a teenager. He started to ignore his owner's commands and he'd bark in the car and in the backyard, but he was never aggressive or really bad, just full of fun and adventurous.

His owner asked one of the instructors for advice and was told he needed to show his dog who was boss. If Jewel was barking in the back of the car, he was told he should stop the car, climb into the back, grab hold of Jewel's neck with both hands and wrestle him to the ground.

Jewel's owner did this for several weeks without much success. Jewel continued to bark; the only difference was that now when his owner stopped the car, Jewel would try to get away as he knew what was coming. Then one day when his owner stopped the car, Jewel bit him on the back of the head.

Jewel's owner rang me in despair asking for my advice. He wanted his good-natured, fun-loving dog back. I told him to stop the aggression immediately. I explained that physical discipline tends to create aggression in a dog and rarely ever solves behavioural problems. I did eventually treat Jewel and found him to be one of the most intelligent dogs I have ever come across.

Maintain your height advantage

A dog's dominance and position in the pack can be based on height. Some dogs will rear up on their opponent in a fight or when playing, in an effort to establish their dominance. The dog that submits will always adopt a lower position than that of the dominant dog. I once saw a female chihuahua dominating a male German shepherd. The shepherd got as close to the ground as possible, showing the smaller dog that he knew she was the boss.

It stands to reason that if you're trying to get your dog to do something and you are at a height disadvantage, you could be bitten. If you are sitting on a sofa with your dog beside you, and for some reason you need to discipline the dog, it might just have a nip at you because it feels superior. In fact, if the dog does not respect your authority, you run the risk of being attacked by your dog in any disciplinary situation where the dog has the height advantage.

Your position might be viewed by the dog as inferior when you are:

- Standing at the foot of the stairs and the dog is higher up the stairs
- Lying down in bed
- Sitting down at the table or on a sofa
- Sitting in the car
- Sitting on the floor

If at any time you feel threatened by your own dog, stand up immediately. Do not smack, point or bend down to the dog. Keep your movements to a minimum and maintain your full height. Use only your voice to stave off attack. Most dogs will back down the minute you re-establish your height dominance.

These instructions are not designed to frighten you into thinking that your own dog will attack you. They are for those of you whose dog is a disciplinary problem. Believe me, there are plenty of dogs like that around. My company attends thousands of such cases each year. One of the more memorable of these was a Rottweiler named Carlo, who took over the top floor of his master's house, biting anyone who tried to make him come downstairs. His story is outlined in the case history below.

Case history: I had been called in to help catch Carlo at the request of the vet, who was unable to get close enough to tranquillise him. When I arrived, most of the family were nursing bites to some part of their anatomy, so you can imagine the type of dog I was confronted with.

At the top of the stairs was the largest Rottweiler I have ever seen. He was facing me with his head lowered and his front legs spread apart and slightly bent. He snarled at me from the top of the stairs.

I asked the owners, Kathy and Bill, if they had any idea why Carlo was behaving this way. Kathy replied: 'It all appeared to start this afternoon when I was getting his bath ready. He's always hated bathtime, but he usually just runs upstairs and hides under the bed. He has tried to bite me before to stop me getting him out from under the bed but I just pushed him out with the broom. Once I get hold of him he's fine and he has his bath without any problems. Today, instead of hiding under the bed, he ran up the stairs and just stood at the top. When we try to get him down he bites us and he won't even let us past.'

I asked Kathy to bring me Carlo's favourite toy and some of his favourite food. 'That won't work,' said Bill. 'Don't you think we've tried all that?'

I ignored his obvious agitation with me and replied, 'I don't want him to come down – not yet, anyway. I want to go up there'.

The family looked at me as if I were insane. I explained that Carlo wouldn't come downstairs because he thought the bath was waiting for him. Because of his height advantage, he was in the position of strength. I needed to get on the same level as him.

I put a lead in my pocket as well as the ball and held the food in my hand as I climbed the stairs. Feeling very vulnerable, I stopped about five stairs from the top. Carlo's face was now level with mine.

His growl had deepened in pitch as I mounted the stairs. He appeared to be very agitated as his eyes stared into mine. I averted my eyes but still kept a close watch on him. I threw some food at his feet. He sniffed it, then returned his concentration to me. I took a step back down the stairs: I wanted him to go for the food. I was halfway down when he gobbled up the food.

I returned to the step I'd been standing on and repeated the process until eventually I could stay where I was. But this wasn't good enough. I needed him to back away from the steps. I needed to get on to the same level as Carlo.

I threw some food behind him, but he didn't move. Suddenly, I had an idea. What if I lowered my height? Perhaps then he would feel more relaxed. I crouched down and threw some food directly behind Carlo. He turned around and grabbed it, then resumed his position. He was not growling at me anymore and seemed much friendlier. Still crouching, I kept repeating this procedure until I was able to throw some food up the hallway. Carlo ran for it. I seized the opportunity and ran up the stairs, keeping as low as I could. I did not want him to see me until I was in position at the top of the stairs.

I don't know who was more bewildered, me or Carlo, when he turned and saw me standing at the top of the stairs. He stood there looking at me, unsure of what I might do next.

I took out his ball and he looked confused. I started bouncing it a couple of times.

I called down the stairs without taking my eyes off Carlo and without missing a bounce. 'What does he normally do when he gets the ball?' A voice came back, 'He will come and drop it at your feet.'

Although I was nervous, I threw the ball up the hallway behind Carlo and he immediately ran to fetch it. He trotted back to me, chewing on the ball and tossing his head from side to side, then dropped the ball at my feet.

About ten throws later it was time for me to take control. I picked up the ball and said, 'Carlo, come', in the most pleasant voice I could muster. I began to take the lead out of my pocket and again shouted down the stairs. 'What do you say to him when you take him for a walk?' One of the children yelled back, 'Mum usually says "walkies" '.

Carlo was now sitting at my feet, looking excitedly at the lead. I told the family that I was taking him for a walk, and to act as if nothing had had happened when we got back.

Carlo enjoyed his walk and I found him to be a very soft-natured and intelligent dog.

So why did Carlo bite his owners?

He hated his bath and everything associated with it. So as soon as he heard water running and his owner calling his name, he would disappear under the bed and bite his owner's hand to stop her grabbing his collar and pulling him out. Humans hit with their hands, dogs hit with their teeth.

When Carlo eventually realised that his hiding place was no good, he decided to try a different approach. Remembering the bad experience with the broom, on this occasion he decided to stop his owner from coming up the stairs. Once he realised he had the upper hand he became more determined not to let the family anywhere near him.

STOPPING A DOG FIGHT

One of the most common situations in which people are bitten is when trying to separate dogs in a fight. A fighting dog has no conscience; it is just as likely to bite you as it is to bite its opponent. Even usually placid dogs have been known to bite their owners when they attempted to break up a fight.

Grabbing a dog in this situation is extremely dangerous, and the results can be horrific. A man in South Australia was fatally wounded trying to separate his pets when they were fighting. Because he was alone with the dogs, he bled to death before help arrived.

You should *never* attempt to break up a fight on your own. Enlist the help of a family member, friend or neighbour. Without getting too close to the dogs, throw a bucket of water at their faces or drench them with a hose. In most cases, the dogs will stop fighting straight away. If not, keep drenching them until they do.

Only experienced dog handlers should attempt to separate the dogs physically. In this case, the handler and their helper each grab one dog's collar and, holding firm, lift the dog's front feet off the ground so it is standing on its hind legs. They then separate the dogs immediately.

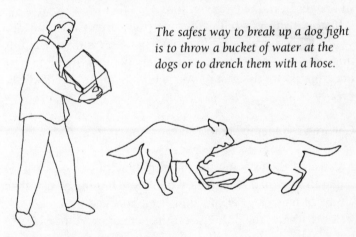

The safest way to break up a dog fight is to throw a bucket of water at the dogs or to drench them with a hose.

DOG-PROOFING CHILDREN

It is vital that all parents, teachers and carers know in what situations dogs represent a real danger to the children in their care. The safety of our children must be paramount in our minds. It is our responsibility to teach them simple, easy-to-remember hints for dealing with dogs.

Many of the techniques that children are encouraged to use are potentially dangerous. Some programs advocate such tips as: ask the owner before you pat a strange dog; make a fist with your fingers and present the back of your clenched fist to the dog; if attacked, stare straight into the dog's eyes. These same programs promote getting children to feed dogs and discipline them.

I believe that all these things are more likely to encourage a dog to bite than prevent it. For example, advising a child to ask the owner before they pat a strange dog is dangerous on several counts. Not only are many people bitten when trying to pat a strange dog but, as we have seen, most dog owners cannot accurately predict what their dogs will do in a particular situation. Not only that, but the child could be in danger from the stranger, too.

In this section, I will show you the correct way to teach your child to deal with dogs, and how to train your family dog to respect your child. If the safety points I highlight here are adhered to, the risk of your child being attacked will be greatly reduced.

Children's vulnerability

Because of their diminutive height, which makes it easy for a dog to bite their face, children are much more at risk than adults of receiving serious injuries if attacked by a dog.

But that's not the only reason they are more vulnerable. As far as a dog is concerned, a child has the same status in the pack as a puppy and therefore it will have no qualms about reprimanding them, yet the same dog would baulk at attacking an adult.

Children are also more impulsive than adults, and are more likely to cuddle and pat a dog. This not only places children at risk of attack from strange dogs but also from their own dog.

How to make the family dog respect your child

Never leave a baby or child alone with a dog

In a pack situation, a mother dog is very protective of her puppies and never allows other dogs near them when they are young. It is not unknown for another dog to perceive a puppy as a threat to its position in the pack, and this can apply just as easily when the pack members are human.

A lady in the United States was visiting a friend and left her newborn baby lying on a sofa in the same room as her friend's chihuahuas. The mother returned a few minutes later to find that the chihuahuas had attacked and killed her child. No female dog would have left her puppies alone in that situation; instinct would have warned her of the dangers. Perhaps the dog's owner had reassured the mother that the dogs were harmless — certainly their size would have supported that impression.

Although what happened in this case is horrific, I don't believe the dogs intended to kill the baby. It is more likely that they were asserting their dominance. However, the victim was a tiny baby and it would not have taken much before the poor little mite succumbed to its injuries.

No matter how much you trust a dog, you cannot predict what will happen if you leave it alone with your child. Your child might do something to upset the dog and, as a reprimand, it might bite your child. Attacks on children are much more common than attacks on adults, and the injuries are more severe.

73

Of course, this does not mean that all domestic dogs will attack a baby if given the chance. The risk of this happening is actually very small, but any risk where a baby is concerned is too great. So the first golden rule is *never leave a baby or child alone with a dog,* even the tiniest dog.

It has been suggested that dogs have an intelligence similar to that of a five-year-old child. Bearing that in mind, just think how long two five-year-olds will play in the backyard before one of them comes in crying 'Mummy, she hit me'. The same thing could happen between a dog and a child, but the difference is dogs hit with their teeth. Remember, you cannot predict what will happen if you leave dogs and children together unattended.

Never allow you dog to snatch food from your child

A female dog in the wild would never allow another dog to take food from her offspring. She'd savagely attack and repel any dog who attempted to do so. This fact would be common knowledge amongst the pack members, one they knew instinctively or had learned through experience. Either way, they would keep well clear of young puppies who had a mother nearby to protect them.

So, the second golden rule is *never allow your dog to steal food from your child.* A dog that's allowed to take toys or food away from children will have little respect for them and won't think twice about snapping if they step out of line (for example, hurting the dog, touching its food, and so on).

When you discipline your dog for this behaviour, you are imitating the way a female dog would protect her young and teaching it that your child must be respected. The dog will soon understand your child has the same status as you.

Your child should always precede the dog through a door or gate

To make certain that your dog has continuing respect for your child, you must ensure that it never dominates them —

ever. By this I mean that all members of the family must enter a room before the dog. If the dog knocks over or pushes past your child, it must be reprimanded immediately.

Don't let your child discipline the dog

Children under twelve years of age should not be allowed to discipline the dog. Most dogs will only treat children with contempt as they cannot show the authority needed. It is far safer to allow only older children and adults to discipline.

Letting a child discipline a dog is akin to a young puppy attempting to dominate an adult dog. It would never happen. Pups will automatically submit to a mature dog, knowing that if they don't, they run the risk of being attacked. I believe the reason many children are attacked is because they don't know the 'pack rules' the way puppies do.

My Doberman Kaydee was recently introduced to my friend's puppy, Cobber. On meeting the pup, Kaydee immediately pounced on him, rolling him onto his back. The pup squealed but made no attempt to jump to his feet; he stayed down, waiting until Kaydee had finished dishing out her disciplinary action. Kaydee didn't bite Cobber — it was all show. It was her way of letting the pup know who was boss, and it worked. Whenever he walked past her, Cobber lowered his head, dropped his tail and grovelled. In this way the pup let Kaydee know she had his respect.

Unfortunately, if a dog decided to discipline a child the way Kaydee disciplined Cobber, the child could be seriously injured. Not understanding the way dogs behave, the child might panic and try to stand up. This would only lead the dog to believe that the child refuses to submit, and so the attack would continue.

To reduce the risk of your child being injured in an attack, teach them to roll into a ball if knocked to the ground by a dog. They should cover their face with their arms and remain as lifeless as possible.

Case history: While at a country dog show in southern New South Wales, I witnessed an horrific attack upon a five-year-old girl called Sarah.

It was an extremely hot, sunny day and I had decided to go for a walk to look at the different breeds that were on show. I had taken a detour through the carpark and I noticed a magnificent-looking collie was tied to a fence with no protection from the hot sun. Concerned for its welfare, I had decided to get the dog a drink when I noticed a young girl walking towards it. It appeared to me that the dog knew the child, as it started wagging its tail as she approached.

Suddenly, the dog's mood changed. It pounced on the child, knocking her to the ground. She screamed and tried to get back on her feet. I sprang into action immediately, running and yelling 'Bah' at the dog as it again pounced on the girl. I was running as fast as I could but I was too far away for the dog to take any notice of me. It continued its attack upon the child, biting her head in an attempt to keep her down.

As I got closer, I could see some blood around her head. I again yelled 'Bah!' as loudly as I could. The dog suddenly realised that I was close and stopped its attack. It cowered down, put its tail between its legs and moved away.

Sarah was taken to hospital suffering from bites to her neck, arms and cheeks. Her trust in dogs was shattered. I later learned that the dog was put to sleep.

This attack took place many years ago before I knew why dogs attacked. Looking back now I realise that the dog must have been fearful of children, judging by its reaction to me. It was possibly stressed by the heat. And of course I now know the wagging tail does not mean the dog was displaying friendship.

In view of its temperament, this dog should never have been tied up where an unsuspecting child could have access to it. The situation could also have been averted if Sarah had been taught to stay away from strange dogs.

Tips for parents

As a parent, it is your responsibility to do all you can to prevent your child being attacked by a dog. The following advice will help keep your child safe:

• Never leave a child alone with a dog.
• When visiting friends or relatives who have a dog, don't allow your child to play in the yard unsupervised. If that's not possible, ask the owners to put the dog away.
• Do not allow your child to feed a dog unsupervised, as some dogs can be very protective of their food.
• Do not allow your child to pull on a dog's collar to lead it outside the house — it could bite them. The dog should be taught to respond to a verbal command.
• Children under eighteen years of age should not be allowed to walk a dog. A child could unwittingly be dragged into a fight with another dog.
• Never buy a dog as a toy substitute. Dogs are living, breathing creatures with feelings. Children should be taught this fact from an early age and shown how to treat dogs with respect.
• Teach your child how to let dogs accept them first by using the techniques in this book.

Obviously, you will not always be around when your child comes into contact with a dog, so it is important that you impress upon them the following rules:

• Never pat a strange dog, even if its owner is present.
• Stay away from a dog while it's eating.
• Stay away from a dog while it's sleeping.
• Stop your bike if chased while riding.
• Never retrieve a ball from someone else's yard.

- If visiting a friend who has a dog, ask them to put the dog away if you want to play.
- Stay away from a dog that has puppies.
- Stay away from a dog that is tied up.
- Never pull a dog's tail or ears — dogs feel pain too.
- Never tease a dog or make it angry.
- Stand totally still if a dog runs at you barking. Cover your face with your hands.
- If knocked to the ground by a dog, roll into a ball, cover your face with your arms and stay as still as you possibly can. Don't try to get up.

Ensure that you teach your child what to do if they are knocked to the ground by a dog. They should roll into a ball, cover their face with their arms and stay as still as possible until help arrives.

TIPS FOR THE ELDERLY

Elderly people are almost as vulnerable as children to a dog attack. Whenever I hear of an attack it concerns me, but attacks on the very young and the elderly upset me the most. If you have an aged person in your family, the hints for protecting children also apply. Be sure they fully understand what to do if attacked by a dog. Question them about what they should do if a dog approaches them. Teach them not to panic or hit out with handbags or umbrellas. Explain that this behaviour will only incite the dog to attack them.

'Dally Says' is a song about a Dalmatian that can talk. He tells children the sort of things that might get them bitten by a dog. The song goes as follows:

Chorus: Do everything Dally says. Doggies won't get a fright and you won't get a bite if you do everything Dally says.

Verse: Stay away from a dog while it's eating, for it might get a fright and you might get a bite so stay away from a dog while its eating.

(repeat chorus)

Never take a toy or a bone from a dog, 'cause it might get a fright and you might get a bite, so never take a toy or a bone from a dog.

(repeat chorus)

Never tease a dog or make it angry, for it might get a fright and you might get a bite, so never tease a dog or make it angry.

(repeat chorus)

Never chase a ball into a strange yard, for doggies might get a fright and you might get a bite, so never chase a ball into a strange yard.

(repeat chorus)

Never pat a strange dog, for it might get a fright and you might get a bite, so never pat a strange dog.

(repeat chorus)

Stop your bike if chased while riding, 'cause he might get a fright and you might get a bite, so stop your bike if chased while riding.

Excerpts from 'Dally Says', a video on dog safety for children. From an original idea by S & D Wilson. Words by Brian Pickering.

Part 3

Handling dogs safely: a guide for professionals

If handling dogs is part of your job, the likelihood of being bitten is high and the rules are somewhat different from those we have so far covered. The environment in which you might be dealing with the dog plays a big part in whether or not a dog is liable to attack: Are you on or off the dog's territory? Are you in the open or in a confined space? Are you examining the dog on a table or on the ground?

Because of these different situations, I have divided this part into two sections. Section 1 is for vets, kennel hands, groomers and the like, and Section 2 is for those of you in the service industry — meter readers, postal workers and door-to-door representatives.

1. VETS, VET NURSES, KENNEL HANDS, ANIMAL SHELTER WORKERS AND GROOMERS

Approaching a dog correctly

When approaching a strange dog and its owner, it is advisable to allow the dog to assess you first. As you approach, don't stare at the dog or attempt to pat or touch it. Talk to the owner calmly, allowing the dog to sniff you if it wants to. Keep your hands in front of you and held close to your body.

Sometimes it is better to ignore the dog until it shows you that it's accepted you. Most people are bitten because they try to rush the initial meeting process with dogs. Believe me, some dogs cannot be rushed; they need time to sniff and assess who or what you are, otherwise they will bite.

If a dog is not going to accept you readily it will usually withdraw or try to hide behind its owner. Pushing a dog too far at this stage by persistently trying to make friends will only add to the dog's fear. If you are talking to the owner in a calm manner the dog will be more likely to accept you because the owner does.

A dog that accepts you will usually push its head up under your hand for a pat. Do not attempt to pat the dog before it has given you this sign.

Taking a dog from the owner

Over the years I have spent a lot of time with dogs, and I've learned there are special ways to handle dogs that lessen the risk of attack. I discovered very early on that it was best if the owner handed the dog to me, rather than if I took the dog from the owner. This often made the difference between whether or not the dog would try to bite me.

One of the women at the RSPCA shelter was very nearly

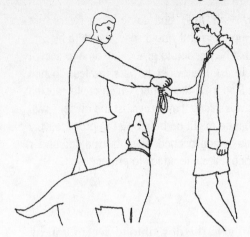

Always ask the owner to hand their dog or the lead to you. This reduces the risk of being attacked, as the dog will not feel like it is being taken away against the owner's will.

bitten on the face by a little dog in its owners arms. The only thing that saved her was her glasses. When the dog snapped at her face it hit her glasses instead. I later took this dog from the owner, but this time I asked her to hand the dog to me, rather than reaching over and taking it from her arms. The dog looked astonished but it made no attempt to bite me.

The same tactic applies if you are dealing with a dog on lead. I was grabbed on the shoulder by a mastiff one day when I attempted to take its lead from the owner. Fortunately, the dog did not bite me; I stood totally still and waited for the owner to release the dog's grip on me.

When a dog's owner hands you the dog (or lead), the dog feels that its owner approves of what's going on and usually does not resist, thereby greatly reducing the risk of attack.

Case history: Neil had been working in a grooming parlour for many years, and was puzzled as to why dogs sometimes bit him. I asked him to tell me how he behaved when a dog was brought into the salon so I could ascertain exactly what he was doing wrong.

Neil said he always approached a dog from the front, and would pat it or take its lead from the owner and try to lead it away.

Mostly he got away with this, but some dogs were not comfortable with his approach and would snap at or bite him.

I explained to Neil that he needed to give a dog time to accept him and that he should ask the owner to pass the lead to him rather than taking the lead from the owner, which could cause a dog to believe that he was taking it away against the owner's will.

I also pointed out that he might be behaving too provocatively by staring at the dog as he approached. This places a dog under pressure and could encourage it to attack to protect itself.

Examining dogs

Again, it is important to give the dog time to accept you by talking to the owner first and allowing the dog to sniff you. Also bear in mind that the dog might have had an unpleasant experience during a similar examination in the past.

I believe most veterinary examination tables are too high, giving the patient a height advantage over the examiner and thereby increasing the risk of an attack. Wherever possible, try to conduct the examination with the dog standing on the ground. This will give you a definite height advantage.

It is advisable to muzzle the dog if examining its eyes, because dogs feel very threatened when you stare into their eyes. (See 'Staring: a provocative act' on page 57.)

Always keep your eye on the dog — it's body language will tell you plenty. (See 'Interpreting a dog's body language' on page 43). A dog that is likely to bite in this situation will be focused on you, tight-lipped with a very tense body and looking for a way out. A dog that is relaxed and unconcerned about you will have a relaxed posture and might be panting.

Dealing with a dog that feels cornered

If a dog is cornered it will feel threatened, and because most veterinary examination rooms are quite small, the risk of a dog feeling trapped is high. Try to involve the owner as much as possible by getting them to hold their dog for you. Try to assess if they are confident and capable of holding the dog firmly. A frightened owner is more likely to cause an attack as the dog will feed off their fear and perhaps bite you.

Handling dogs in cages

A frightened dog shut in a small cage will usually feel threatened. If you need to administer treatment to the dog or remove it from the cage and the cage is at face height, the dog will have the height advantage and therefore the upper hand. When dealing with dogs in this situation, stand on a chair or step ladder to give yourself the advantage.

Removing a dog from a car

When transporting a dog, it is imperative to secure the dog in the back of the car with a harness or a dog safety belt. If neither of these is available, it is possible to use two leads attached to the dog's collar, which can be tied to the seat belt anchors or handles above the window on either side of the car. This prevents the dog from becoming tangled in the lead as well as making it easier to control. When you remove the dog from the car, you are able to take hold of one lead while the dog is secured by the other. If a dog should jump at you, hold the lead at arm's length — this will protect you from any snapping teeth. Whenever possible, it's better for the owner to tie the dog in the car.

Make sure you have a doggy treat with you when collecting and dropping off dogs. Simply throw the food at a dog's feet if it becomes aggressive and wait for its mood to change.

When removing a dog from the back of a van, remember the importance of height advantage. You might be better off climbing into the van and asserting this advantage than staying outside and trying to remove the dog that way.

Finally, bear in mind that the dog you are dealing with might feel frightened or trapped. It may even be car-protective, as illustrated in the following case history.

Case history: When I was working for the RSPCA, the police contacted me asking for help. A Rottweiler called Sabre would not let his owner get back in his car, and things were getting desperate. When I arrived at the scene, Sabre was sitting in the back of the car looking very pleased with himself, but growling whenever the owner or the police tried to get him out. Using a catching pole, I was able to transfer Sabre from the car to my RSPCA van relatively easily, but I was concerned about how I was going to get him out once I got back to the shelter.

I was certain that by adopting a non-confrontational approach, I would be able to get Sabre to leave the van quietly. Over the years I had learned that a dog that is behaving aggressively will become even more aggressive if you attempt to invade its space. By the time we arrived back at the shelter Sabre appeared to be relaxed and happy. I opened the rear door of the van and he came up to me with his tail wagging and a friendly look on his face. He showed no sign at all of his previous aggression.

As it turned out, Sabre was car-protective. He hadn't been with his owner very long and had not had time to accept his authority. The previous owner had trained Sabre to guard his car, and Sabre thought he was just doing his job.

2. METER READERS, POSTAL WORKERS AND OTHER DOOR-TO-DOOR REPRESENTATIVES

It may seem that people in these types of jobs are less at risk of attack than a vet, for example, because they are not obliged to handle dogs. However, according to statistics, this is not the case. I believe that fear of the unknown is responsible for the high incidence of dog attacks in the service industry. Many of these people do not own a dog, are afraid of them or simply do not like them. I also believe that the tales and gossip they pass on to each other adds to the paranoia of many service industry and door-to-door representatives. During my research into the problems they face, I met with many people in the industry and found that the lunch room talk mainly centred around dogs.

Participants in these conversations appeared to be divided into three categories. There were those who knew nothing or very little about dogs, and they listened to anyone that they thought had the answers. The second group had their own theories based on half-truths. They led the others to believe they had all the answers and convinced them that aggression was the only way to avoid attack, even though they themselves had been bitten on several occasions. The third group were less vocal, but had for years instinctively practised a technique identical to mine without realising that's why they never got bitten.

One of the main problems I unearthed in this industry was the widespread belief that aggression is the answer. This was partly because of the lunchtime stories about how a certain person in the organisation was able to scare off an aggressive dog by picking up a stick, a rock or drop-kicking the dog. Because the dog in this case ran away, the technique appeared to be successful. However, a dog that runs away is not the type of dog that's likely to launch an attack. A dog with more courage that does not scare easily would not respond to an aggressive technique by fleeing — it would attack.

Safe property entry

Always check to see if there is a dog on the property

Look for signs such as dirty marks on the verandah, caused by the oil from a dog's coat, which leaves a tell-tale sign on wood and fibro.

Entering gates

When entering a gate be aware that a dog could be lurking on the other side waiting for some unsuspecting person to stick their hand over the top of the gate to open it. If you rattle the gate it will usually produce a bark from the dog, indicating to you that a dog is on the property and you need to be on your guard. Always study the dog's body language before entering the property. (See 'Interpreting a dog's body language' on page 43.)

If you don't know whether or not there is a dog lurking in someone's backyard, rattle the gate before entering. The dog will bark, thereby alerting you to its presence.

Knocking on doors

Be aware that some people keep their dog inside the house, so you might not receive a warning bark. If there is a screen door, place your foot against the base of it to prevent a dog from accidentally springing the catch and being able to attack you.

Sandra, who worked for the Australian Electoral Commission, received the fright of her life when she knocked on a door one day. A large malamute came charging at her, as soon as the door was opened, crashing through the screen door and taking it off its hinges. Sandra landed flat on her back and the dog landed on top of her, the screen door firmly wedged between them. The dog just stood there licking her face.

If held in front of you, a large briefcase, a bag, a clipboard or a thick coat can protect you in an attack situation. Do not use it as a weapon — under no circumstances should you swing anything towards a charging dog.

Do not be aggressive
If you behave aggressively towards a dog you will only make the dog more aggressive. Even if it isn't aggressive towards you because you have it bluffed, it may be towards your workmates. By behaving aggressively you are playing with dynamite. One day you will come across a dog that won't back down.

Do not believe the owner
Most dog owners have no concept of what their dog will do under certain circumstances. If you have to enter a property in the course of your work, politely ask the owner to put away their dog while you are there.

If you have to enter a property in the course of your work, politely ask the owner to lock up their pet while you are there. The owner may protest that their dog is not aggressive, but the fact is that no one can predict exactly what their dog will do in certain circumstances.

89

I recently had to have the battery changed on my car. When the mechanic arrived he asked me to put my dog away while he worked on my car. Instinctively, I started to defend my dog and explain that he would not bite, but I stopped myself short, realising that I was not practising what I preached. The man went on to tell me that he had previously been attacked by a dog when he touched its owner's car. He knew first-hand how protective dogs can be of their owner's property.

There are several situations in which you could be bitten when on a property with both dog and owner. For instance, if shaking hands or handing something to the owner, the dog might view this as a threat to its owner and could attack. A dog and its owner equal a potentially dangerous combination, so always keep your eye on the dog's and the owner's movements.

When leaving a property, never turn your back on the dog. They often view leaving as a back-down and might just take the opportunity to give you a sneaky bite to send you on your way.

Case history: Des attended a property one day to disconnect the electricity supply because of an unpaid account. When he arrived he was met by the owner and his bull terrier. The man said he had decided to pay the account and went inside to get a cheque. He returned a short time later and as Des leaned towards him to accept the cheque, the dog leapt at Des, grabbing his arm.

Fortunately, Des did not recoil; he lowered his arm to the ground, going with the dog's movements as it landed back on its feet. The owner released the dog's grip and Des was unharmed.

Do not stare

Never, under any circumstances, should you stare at a dog. It will only incite it to attack if it's feeling uneasy about you. Staring is seen as a threatening and challenging act by dogs.

Dominant dogs will stare at other dogs and submissive, non-challenging dogs will avert their eyes to avoid confrontation.

Maintain your height advantage
If you are sitting or kneeling down and a dog approaches, stand up immediately. Do not move until the dog has had a chance to assess you. If the dog attacks, follow the Stand Right No Bite technique.

Always carry food
I have found that people who use the food approach receive a very positive response from dogs. Many previously aggressive dogs are soon pacified once they are given something to eat.

It is best to carry dry food that fits easily into your pocket, such as dog biscuits or kibble. When the dog approaches you, throw some food on the ground. Do not attempt to pat the dog, but speak to it in a soft voice. You want it to recognise your voice and remember the food next time you visit.

Tips for bike riders

If you ride a motorcycle or pushbike to deliver the mail or papers, for instance, you are in a potentially more dangerous situation than anyone else. Can you imagine just what a dog sees? A thing with two wheels, two legs that kick out at them, two arms and a head — definitely not like a human being at all.

The best way to prevent an attack in this situation is to always carry food. If a dog chases you, stop, get off the bike and remove your helmet. Stand up straight to assert your height dominance then throw some food on the ground for the dog. If it attacks you, use your bike to protect yourself.

Do not behave aggressively or try to kick the dog when you get back on the bike. It will only make the situation worse.

Using electronic devices

These are electronic devices which omit a high-frequency sound when activated. A few years ago these were hailed as the 'cure all' of dog attacks. However, many service industries have now dispensed with them in favour of staff education.

One meter reader told me that on his first day at work he was given a kit which contained a zapper. He said he felt like Billy the Kid. Whenever a dog came running he'd activate the zapper and the dog would flee. He thought, 'This is great, no dog will touch me'.

This approach worked well, until one day when he was reading a meter, a large dog came running round the corner, barking at him. He pointed the zapper at the dog and pressed the button. The dog kept coming. He threw the zapper at it and leapt over the fence.

In my experience, these devices only work on dogs that lack the confidence to attack anyway. Confident, aggressive dogs tend to become even more aggressive.

Remember, an aggressive approach is *always* dangerous, and only increases your chances of being attacked.

Author's note

The reasons why a dog will attack are numerous. In order to dispel the myths, avoid media hype and to prevent anxiety about certain breeds, I firmly believe there should be a dog control organisation in each state, responsible for investigating every attack a dog makes on a person. This would enable the collection and production of accurate information as to why attacks occur. It would also assist law makers to develop sensible legislation based on fact rather than supposition. As I write this, some members of parliament are proposing legislation which will make it a legal requirement for all dog owners to train their dogs. This, I feel, is a more realistic approach to dog control than banning certain breeds.

Keep in mind that humans hit with their hands and dogs with their teeth. When a person attacks another person, the attacker is brought to trial, all the facts are investigated and a reason behind the assault sought. Unfortunately, a dog that attacks a person is usually disposed of as quickly as possible and no defence is offered. If we knew the reasons behind each attack, we would then be able to reduce their number.

Case history: I received a call from the police asking me to assess Bandit, an eighteen-month-old cattle dog accused of attacking three children while they were playing in a park. As a result of the attack, his owner Kelly was charged with owning a savage dog and was soon to appear in court. If she lost the case it would cost Bandit his life.

I rang Kelly and made an appointment to see Bandit the following day. She told me that he had attacked the children without provocation and with considerable frenzy. The children's mother had lifted them onto a slippery dip to keep them out of Bandit's reach. Kelly also said that her two teenage sons had been in charge of Bandit when he attacked, and that they didn't have him on a lead at the time.

When I first met Bandit he was behind a chainwire fence. He flew at the fence, growling, snapping and continually looking over his shoulder, displaying all the signs of a fearful dog.

I sat down with Kelly and asked her many questions. First I wanted to know if she definitely wanted to keep him. I needed to know how seriously she would be committed to his rehabilitation. I also asked who normally walked him, if he had been given any formal training, and how much control she and her sons had over Bandit.

Kelly turned out to be a very devoted dog owner. She told me that Bandit had had no formal training. She loved him, wanted desperately to keep him, and would do everything I told her if it was going to save her dog's life. She also told me the boys were the only ones who walked Bandit and that they had very little control over him, as demonstrated on the day of the attack.

I asked Kelly to go into the backyard with Bandit while I approached the house from the street again. I wanted to see if I could show her how to gain greater control over him. That day, I was able to teach Kelly to communicate with her dog in a way that he could understand and to get the message through to him that she did not approve of his aggression.

I filled out my report to the police the next day. In part, it read as follows:

It is my belief that Bandit is of a fearful nature and that his fear was possibly aggravated by the inexperience of the children. I suggest that in order to prevent an occurrence of the same problem, the following procedures must be adhered to:

1. Bandit should receive extensive obedience training.
2. No person under eighteen years of age should walk or be placed in charge of Bandit outside his property.

3. The dog in question should at all times be walked on lead and should be muzzled when outside the property.
4. Any form of aggression by Bandit should be met with disapproval by his owners.

I recommend that I should be asked to do a follow-up assessment in six weeks' time.

At her court appearance one week later, Kelly was fined $400 and instructed to abide by the recommendations in my report.

When I reassessed Bandit six weeks later, I was elated by his improvement. He was no longer displaying the signs of a fearful dog; instead, he was relaxed and friendly, even allowing me to pat him. As long as Kelly kept him under strict control and maintained the training, I knew Bandit would be unlikely to attack someone ever again.

As this case history shows, it is possible to rehabilitate an aggressive dog. I am aware that some of you may be horrified that I am advocating such a radical approach, but experience has taught me that a dog with a history of aggressive behaviour can be rehabilitated if the owner is totally committed to maintaining strict control and training. The onus always lies with the dog's owner — no dog can be held accountable for its actions. Remember, dogs are pets, and by choosing to own a dog, we have to accept responsibility for its behaviour.

For more help and advice from

Call toll-free on
1800 067 710